DOLLAR BILL ANIMALS
IN ORIGAMI

Other books by John Montroll:

Origami Sculptures

Prehistoric Origami *Dinosaurs and Other Creatures*

Origami Sea Life by John Montroll and Robert J. Lang

African Animals in Origami

Origami Inside-Out

North American Animals in Origami

Mythological Creatures and the Chinese Zodiac in Origami

Teach Yourself Origami

Bringing Origami to Life

Animal Origami for the Enthusiast

Origami for the Enthusiast

Easy Origami

Birds in Origami

Favorite Animals in Origami

DOLLAR BILL ANIMALS IN ORIGAMI

Dover Publications, Inc.
New York

THE NATIONAL ORIGAMI TREASURY

JOHN MONTROLL

To Tim, Jennifer, and Tim

Bibliographical Note

This work is first published in 2000 in separate editions by Antroll Publishing Company, Maryland, and Dover Publications, Inc., New York.

Library of Congress Cataloging-in-Publication Data

Montroll, John.
    Dollar bill animals in origami / John Montroll.
        p. cm.
    ISBN 0-486-41157-5 (pbk.)
    1. Origami. 2. Dollar, American. 3. Animals in art. I. Title.

TT870 .M5533 2000
736'.982—dc21

00-026261

Manufactured in the United States of America
Dover Publications, Inc., 31 East 2nd Street, Mineola, N.Y. 11501

INTRODUCTION

Dollar bill folds have become very popular in origami. The paper is of good folding quality; its size, proportions, and even colors make it an interesting medium to use. You can learn how to fold a wealth of projects including a shark, turtle, apatosaurus, deer, and 28 other models.

Dollar bill folds have been a novelty for some time. Magicians often used them for tricks, stunning audiences who knew that whatever happened, cutting could not be involved. As origami developed in this country, many folders took to the dollar bill because it folds well, has always been available, and has a very adaptable rectangular shape.

I have enjoyed designing these models. Though I generally fold from squares, the dollar bill has an interesting proportion that lends itself well to animal design. In some ways, it is easier to fold animals from rectangles than from squares because animals' bodies are inherently long, allowing for more efficiency from a rectangle.

It is up to you which side of the dollar bill should show in finished models. Although the diagrams use white and shading to represent the dollar bill's two sides, you may choose which side of the actual bill you wish to show; generally, the diagrams will show predominantly the shaded side. However, the final drawings of each model are completely shaded and do not distinguish between the two sides.

Of course you do not need to fold from dollar bills. Any paper can easily be cut to form the proportions of a bill. My favorite method, shown on page 10, shows an easy way to approximate the proportions given a square or rectangle. The illustrations conform to the internationally accepted Randlett-Yoshizawa conventions. Origami paper can be found in many hobby shops or purchased by mail from OrigamiUSA, 15 West 77th Street, New York, NY 10024-5192 or from Dover Publications, Inc., 31 East 2nd Street, Mineola, NY 11501. Large sheets are easier to use than small ones.

I wish to thank the origami community for encouraging me to write this book. Also I thank the printers Port City Press, Inc. for a decade of service. Thanks to my editors, Jeremy and Josh Korr. Of course I also thank the many folders who proof-read the diagrams.

John Montroll

CONTENTS

Symbols   9
Dollar Bills from a Square   10
Basic Folds   118

★   Simple
★★   Intermediate
★★★   Complex

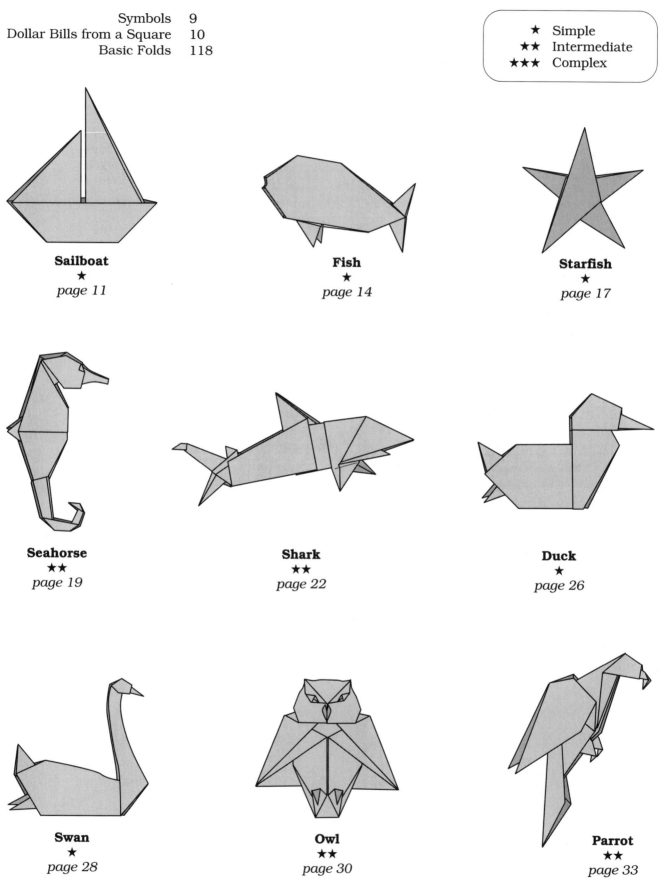

Sailboat
★
page 11

Fish
★
page 14

Starfish
★
page 17

Seahorse
★★
page 19

Shark
★★
page 22

Duck
★
page 26

Swan
★
page 28

Owl
★★
page 30

Parrot
★★
page 33

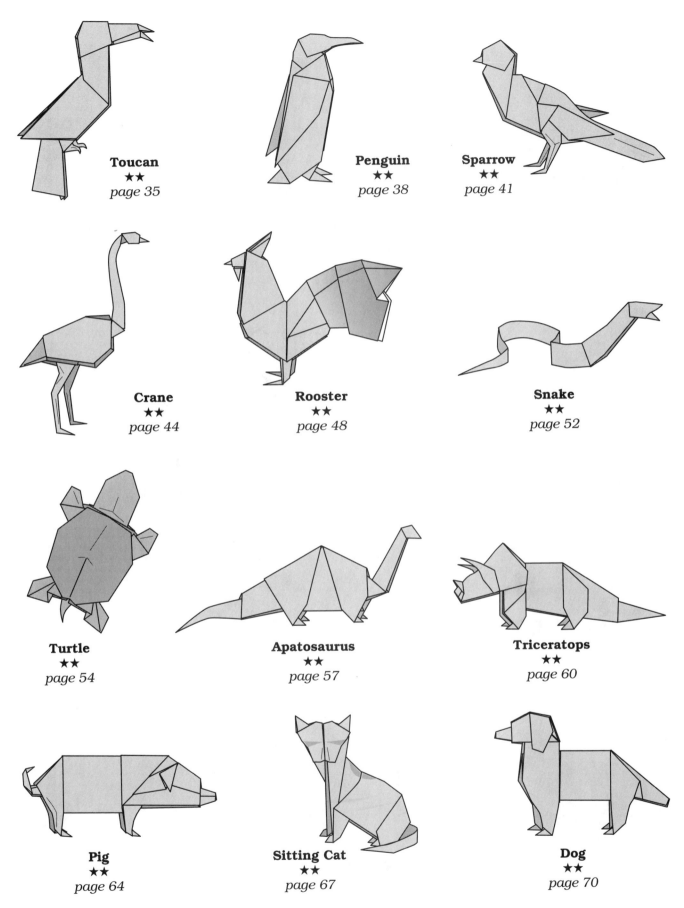

Toucan
★★
page 35

Penguin
★★
page 38

Sparrow
★★
page 41

Crane
★★
page 44

Rooster
★★
page 48

Snake
★★
page 52

Turtle
★★
page 54

Apatosaurus
★★
page 57

Triceratops
★★
page 60

Pig
★★
page 64

Sitting Cat
★★
page 67

Dog
★★
page 70

More →

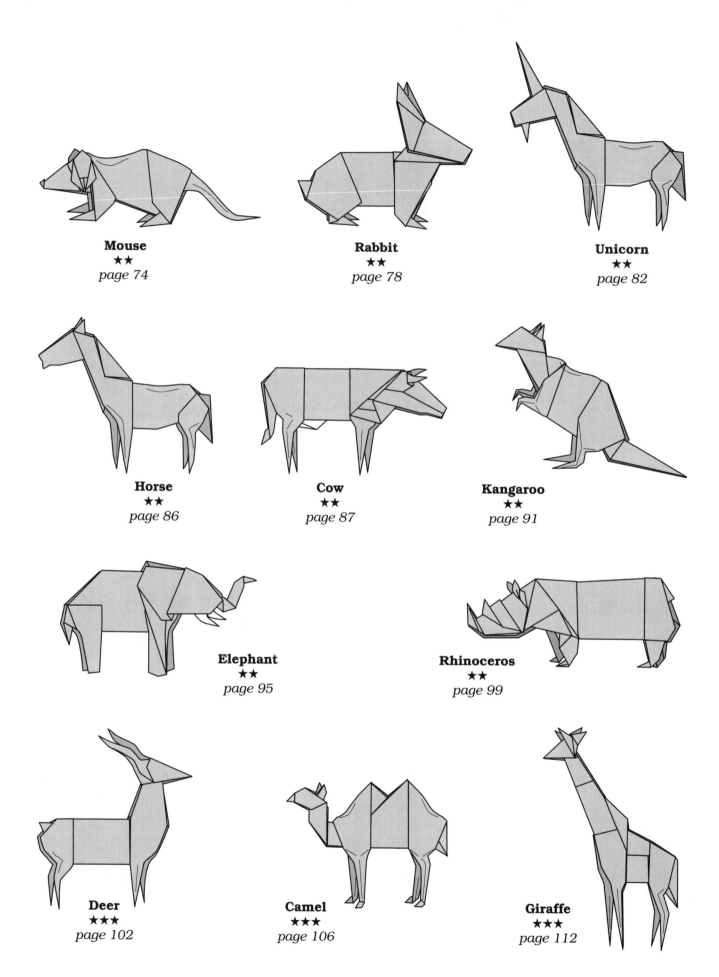

Mouse
★★
page 74

Rabbit
★★
page 78

Unicorn
★★
page 82

Horse
★★
page 86

Cow
★★
page 87

Kangaroo
★★
page 91

Elephant
★★
page 95

Rhinoceros
★★
page 99

Deer
★★★
page 102

Camel
★★★
page 106

Giraffe
★★★
page 112

SYMBOLS

Lines

— — — — — — — — — Valley fold, fold in front.

—·—·—·—·—·—·—·— Mountain fold, fold behind.

——————————— Crease line.

····················· X-ray or guide line.

Arrows

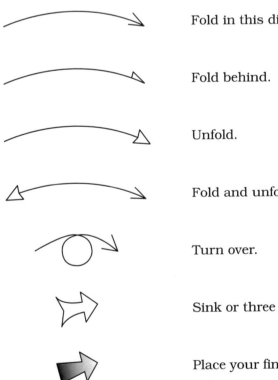

Fold in this direction.

Fold behind.

Unfold.

Fold and unfold.

Turn over.

Sink or three dimensional folding.

Place your finger between these layers.

DOLLAR BILLS FROM A SQUARE

The dollar bill has dimensions of approximately 2.59 inches by 6.094 inches. This ratio is 1 by 2.35. There are two simple, approximate methods of cutting any square or rectangle to have the proportions of a dollar bill. One is to use the dimensions 3 by 7 (1 by 2.333). Another method is to create a rectangle with the diagonal at a 22.5° angle as shown here; the ratio for this method is approximately 1 by 2.414.

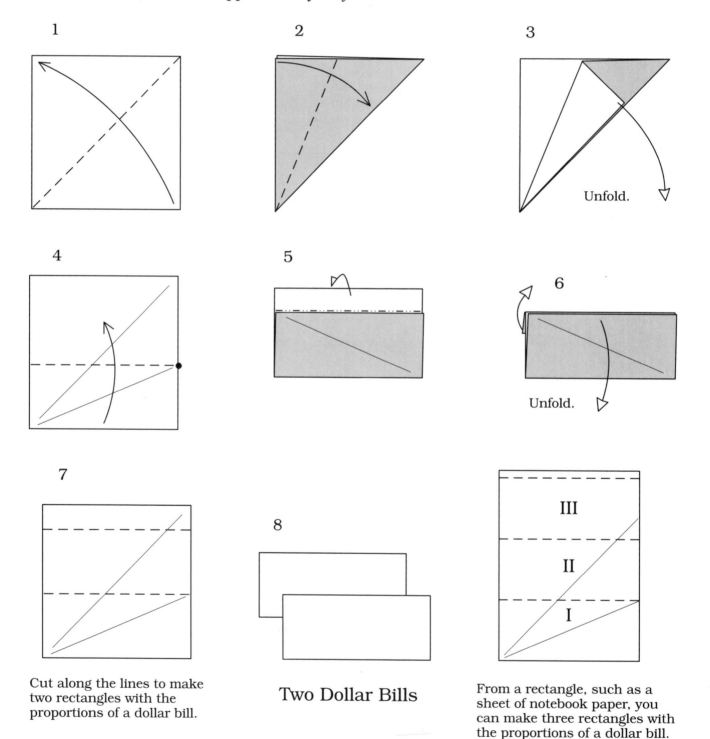

1

2

3

Unfold.

4

5

6

Unfold.

7

8

III

II

I

Cut along the lines to make two rectangles with the proportions of a dollar bill.

Two Dollar Bills

From a rectangle, such as a sheet of notebook paper, you can make three rectangles with the proportions of a dollar bill.

SAILBOAT

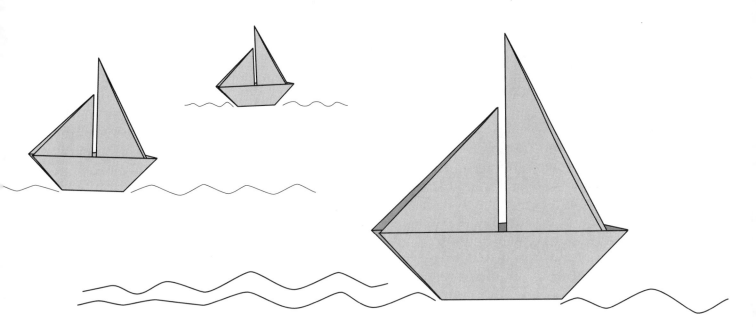

1

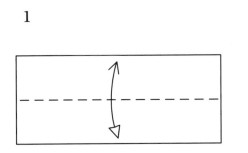

Fold and unfold.

2

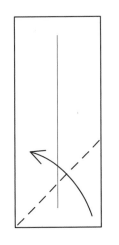

3

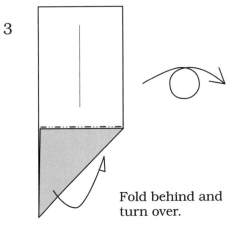

Fold behind and
turn over.

4

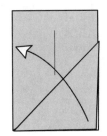

Unfold.

5

6

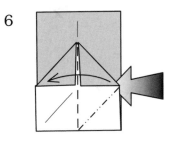

Squash-fold.

7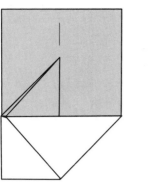

8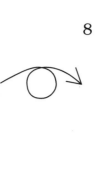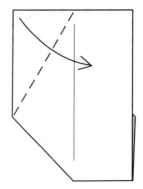

9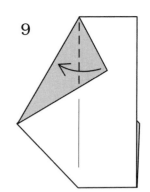

10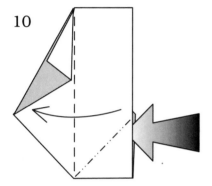

Squash-fold.

11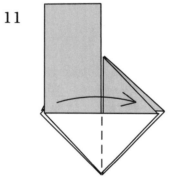

12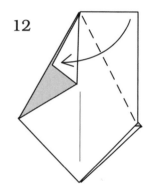

13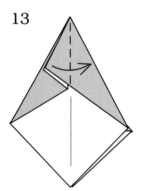

14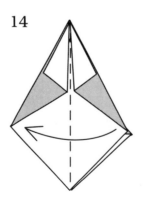

15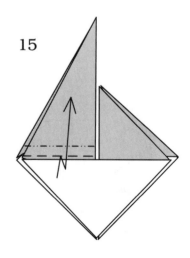

Fold down and up.

16

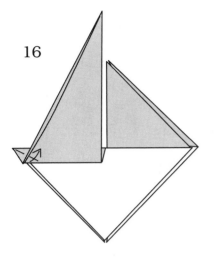

17

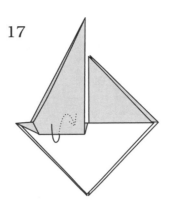

Tuck the bottom of the sail
under the white paper.

18

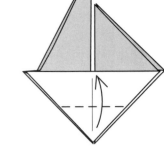

19

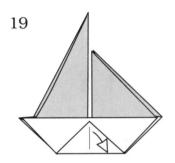

Fold the triangle down a
little to act as the stand.

Or

20

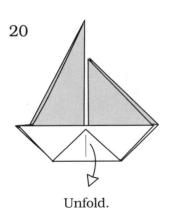

Unfold.

21

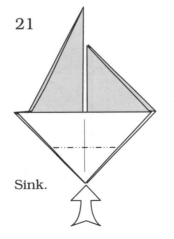

Sink.

20

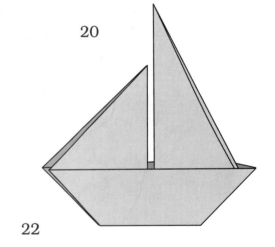

22

Sailboat

FISH

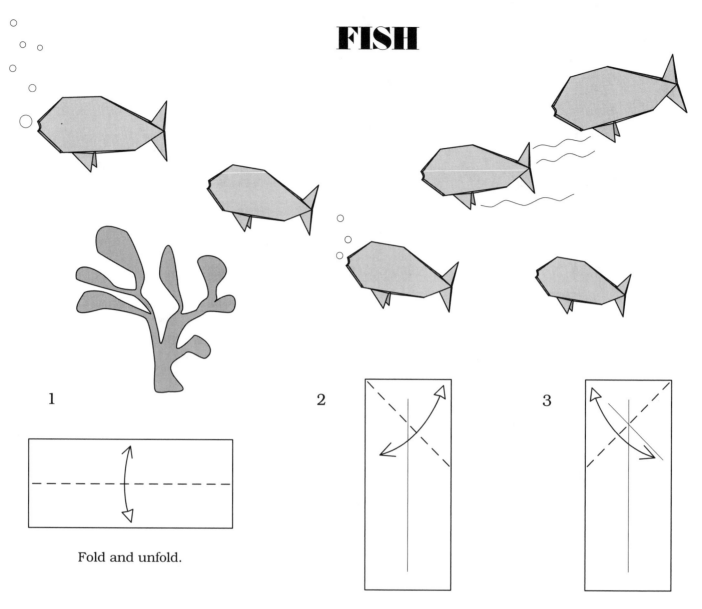

1

Fold and unfold.

2

Fold and unfold.

3

Fold and unfold.

4

5

6

Unfold.

7

8

9

Unfold.

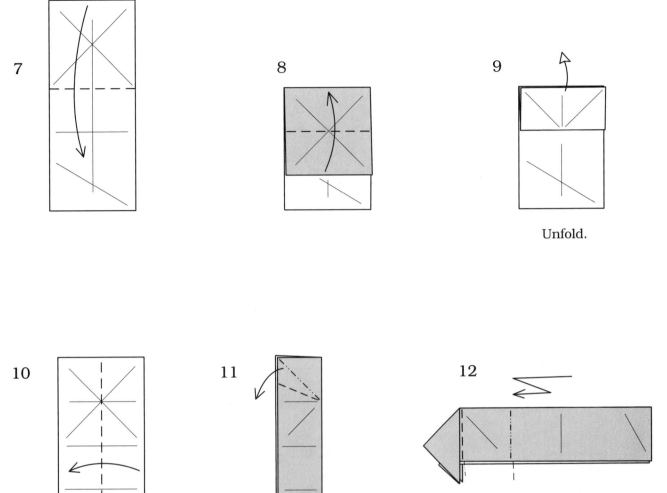

10

11

Crimp-fold and rotate.

12

Two reverse folds.

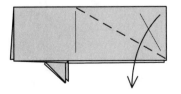

13

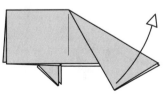

14

Unfold.

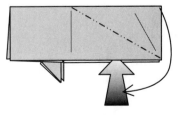

15

Reverse-fold.

Fish 15

16

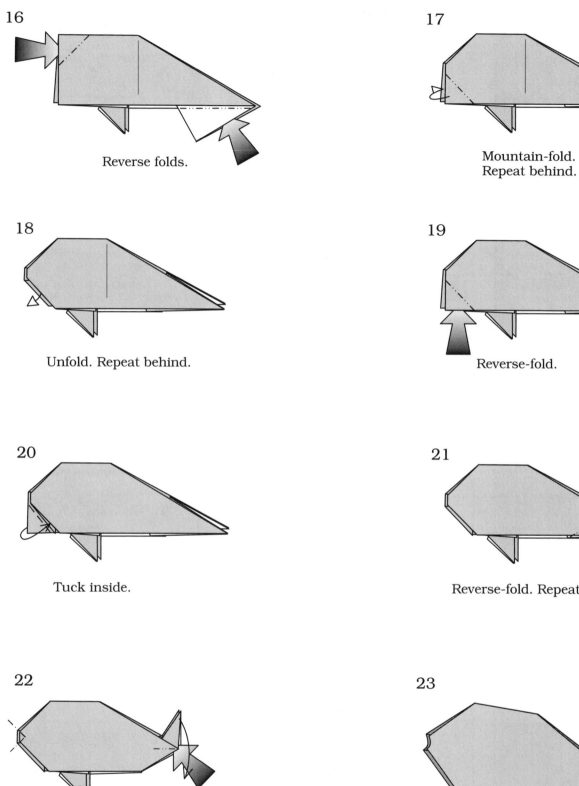

Reverse folds.

17

Mountain-fold.
Repeat behind.

18

Unfold. Repeat behind.

19

Reverse-fold.

20

Tuck inside.

21

Reverse-fold. Repeat behind.

22

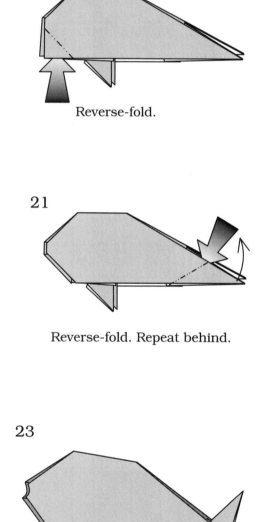

Reverse-fold the tail, shape the
mouth, and spread the fins.

23

Fish

STARFISH

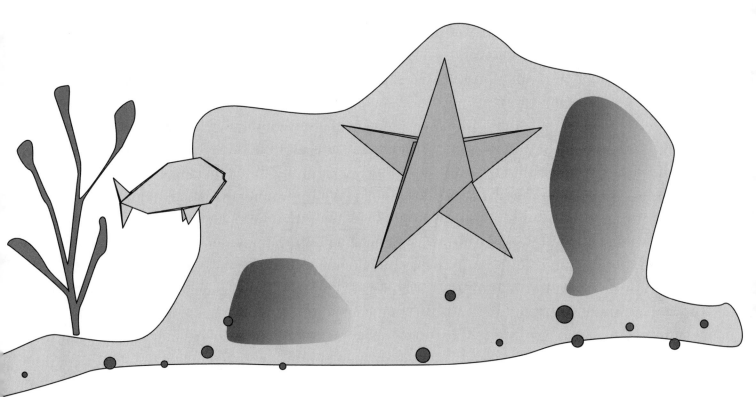

1

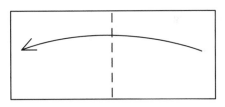

2

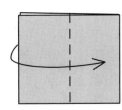

Fold both layers.

3

Unfold.

4

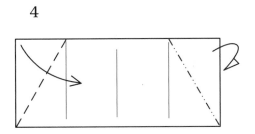

5

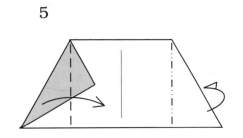

6

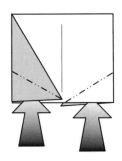

Reverse-folds.

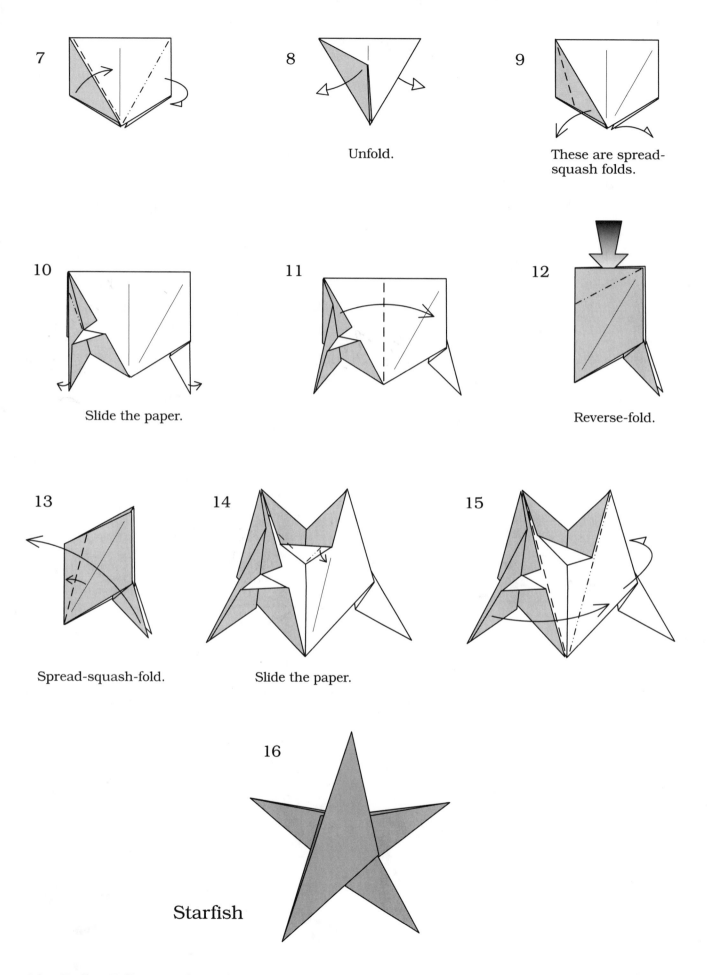

7

8

Unfold.

9

These are spread-squash folds.

10

Slide the paper.

11

12

Reverse-fold.

13

Spread-squash-fold.

14

Slide the paper.

15

16

Starfish

SEAHORSE

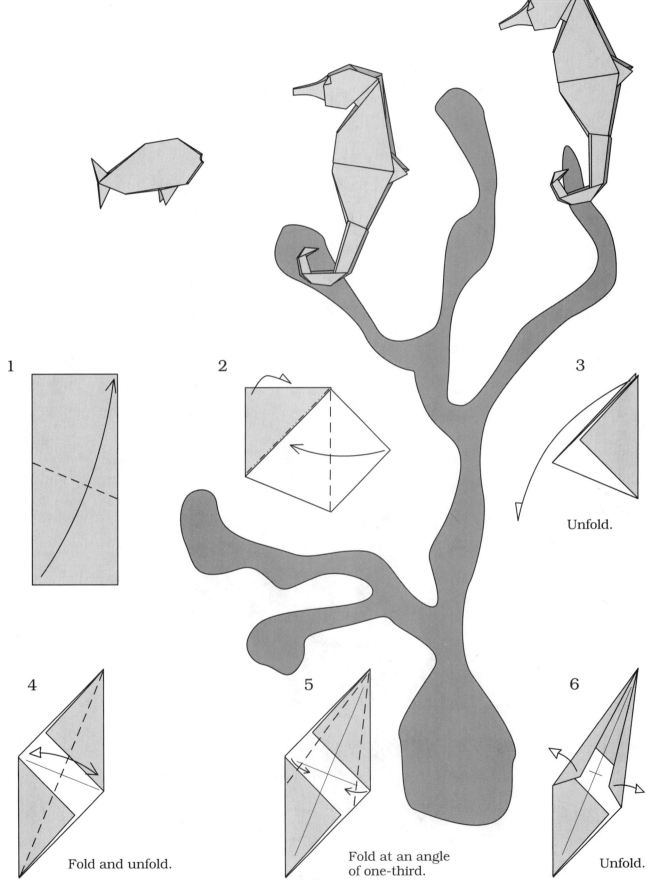

1

2

3

Unfold.

4

Fold and unfold.

5

Fold at an angle
of one-third.

6

Unfold.

7

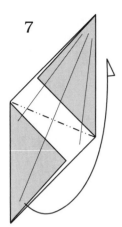

8

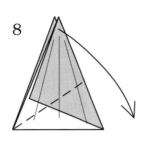

9

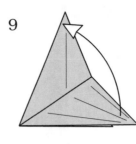

Unfold.

10

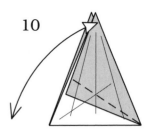

Fold and unfold.

11

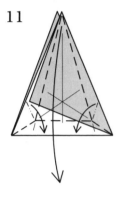

12

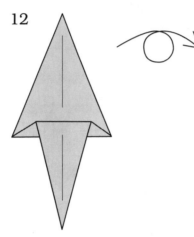

13

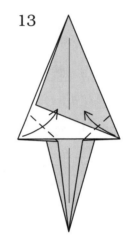

14

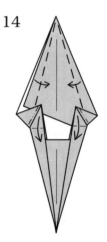

Squash folds.

15

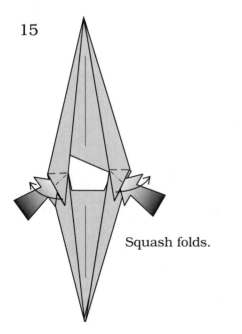

Squash folds.

16

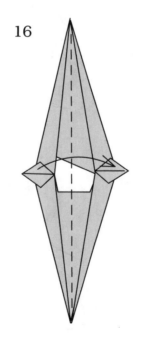

17

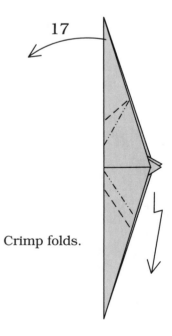

Crimp folds.

18

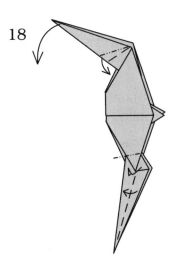

Crimp-fold the head.
Repeat behind at the tail.

19

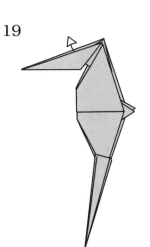

Pull out.
Repeat behind.

20

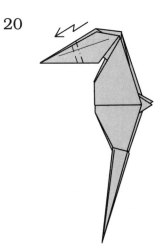

Crimp-fold.

21

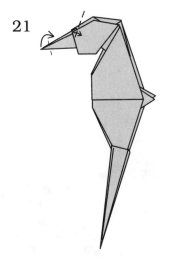

Reverse-fold the nose.
Repeat behind for the eyes.

22

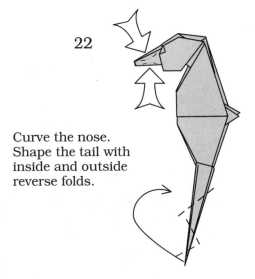

Curve the nose.
Shape the tail with
inside and outside
reverse folds.

23

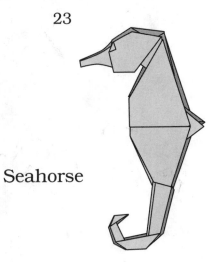

Seahorse

SHARK

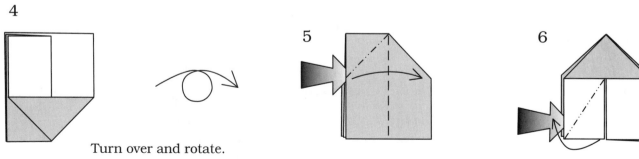

1

Fold and unfold.

2

3

Squash-fold.

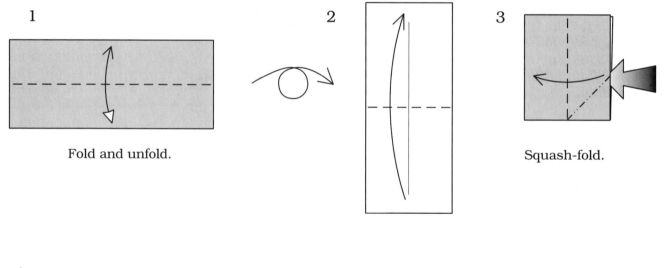

4

Turn over and rotate.

5

Squash-fold.

6

Reverse-fold.

7

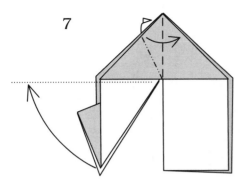

Crimp-fold to the dotted line.

8

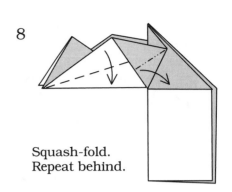

Squash-fold.
Repeat behind.

9

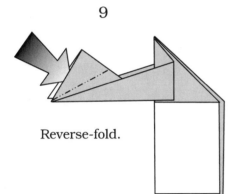

Reverse-fold.

10

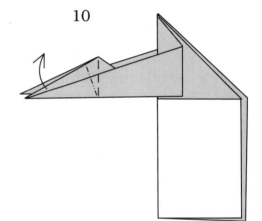

11

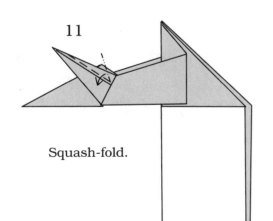

Squash-fold.

12

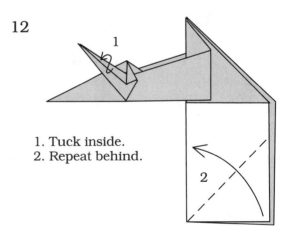

1. Tuck inside.
2. Repeat behind.

13

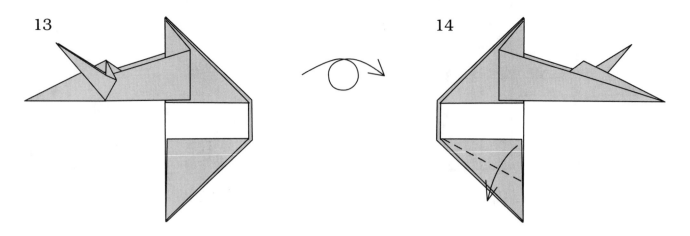

14

Do not repeat behind.

15

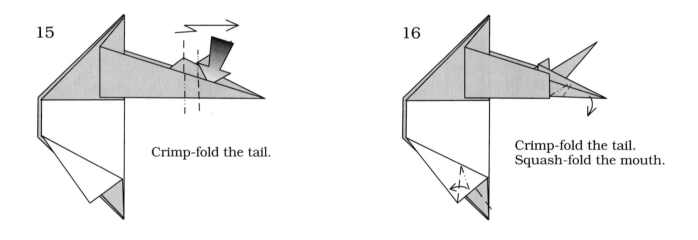

Crimp-fold the tail.

16

Crimp-fold the tail.
Squash-fold the mouth.

17

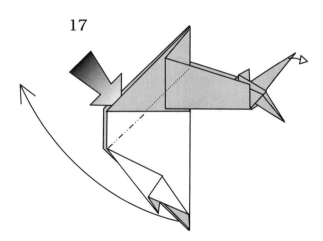

Spread the tip of the tail.
Reverse-fold at the front.

18

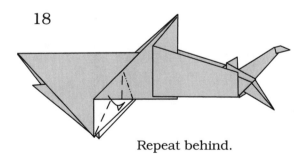

Repeat behind.

19

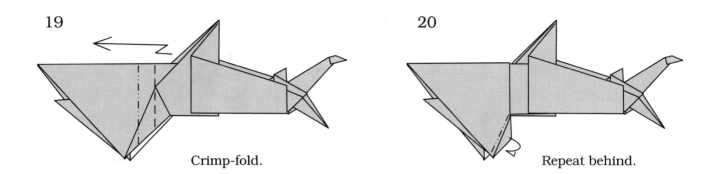

Crimp-fold.

20

Repeat behind.

21

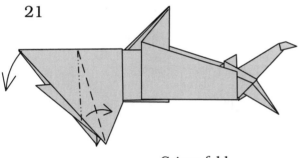

Crimp-fold.

22

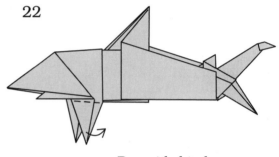

Repeat behind.

23

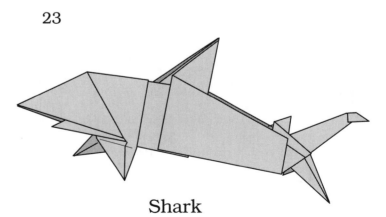

Shark

DUCK

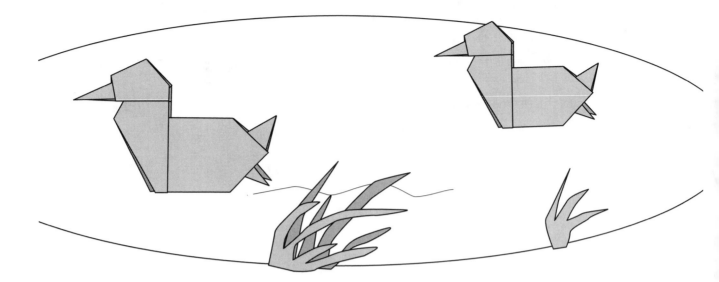

1

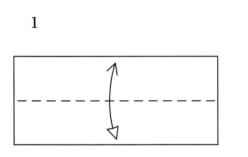

Fold and unfold.

2

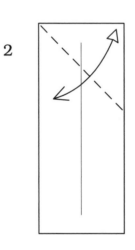

Fold and unfold.

3

Fold and unfold.

4

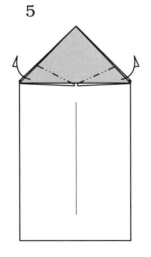

5

6

Squash folds.

7

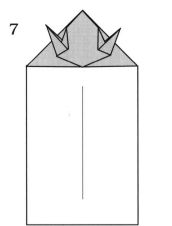

8

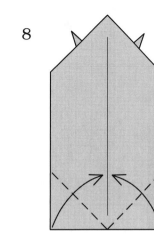

9

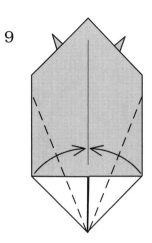

10

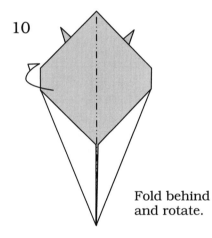

Fold behind
and rotate.

11

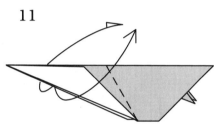
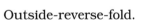

Outside-reverse-fold.

12

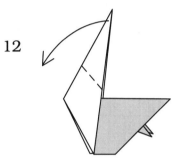

Outside-reverse-fold.

13

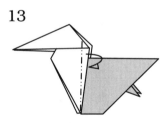

Repeat behind.

14

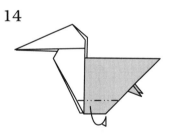

Repeat behind.

15

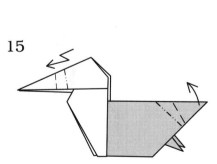

Crimp folds.

16

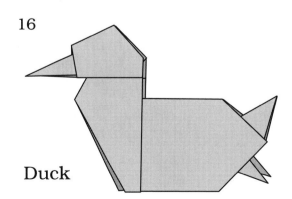

Duck

SWAN

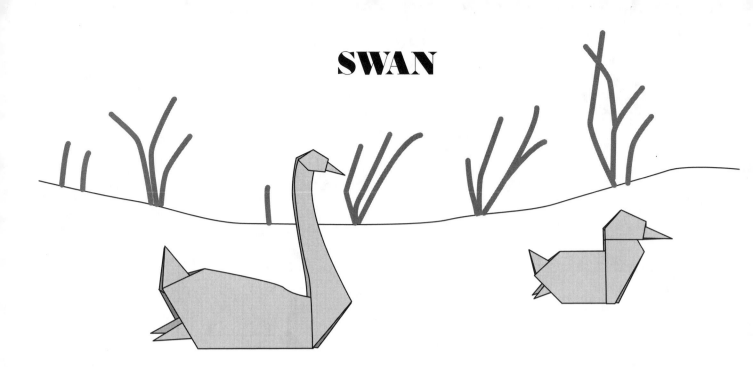

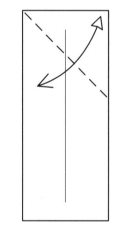

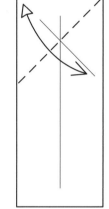

1

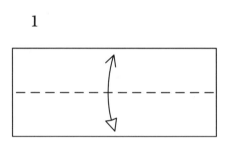

Fold and unfold.

2

Fold and unfold.

3

Fold and unfold.

4

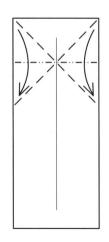

5

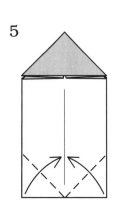

6

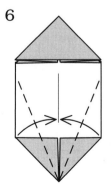

7

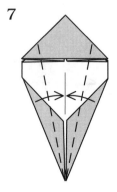

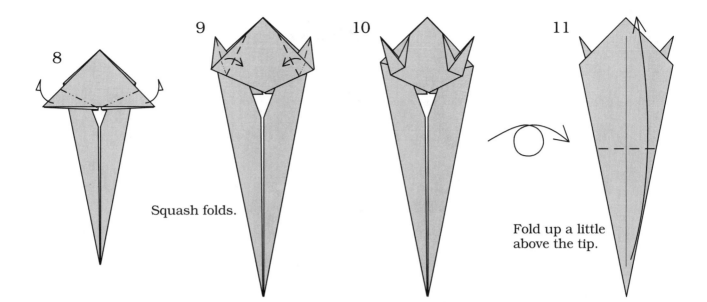

8

9

Squash folds.

10

11

Fold up a little above the tip.

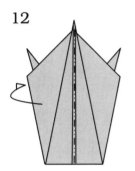

12

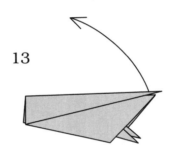

13

Slide the neck up.

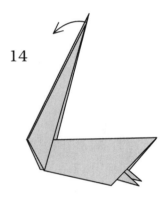

14

Open the head.

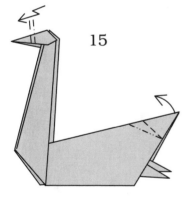

15

Crimp folds.

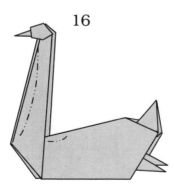

16

Curve the neck.

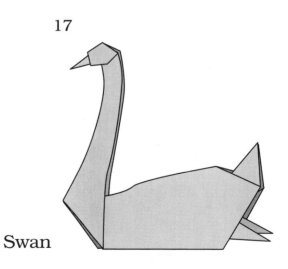

17

Swan

Swan 29

OWL

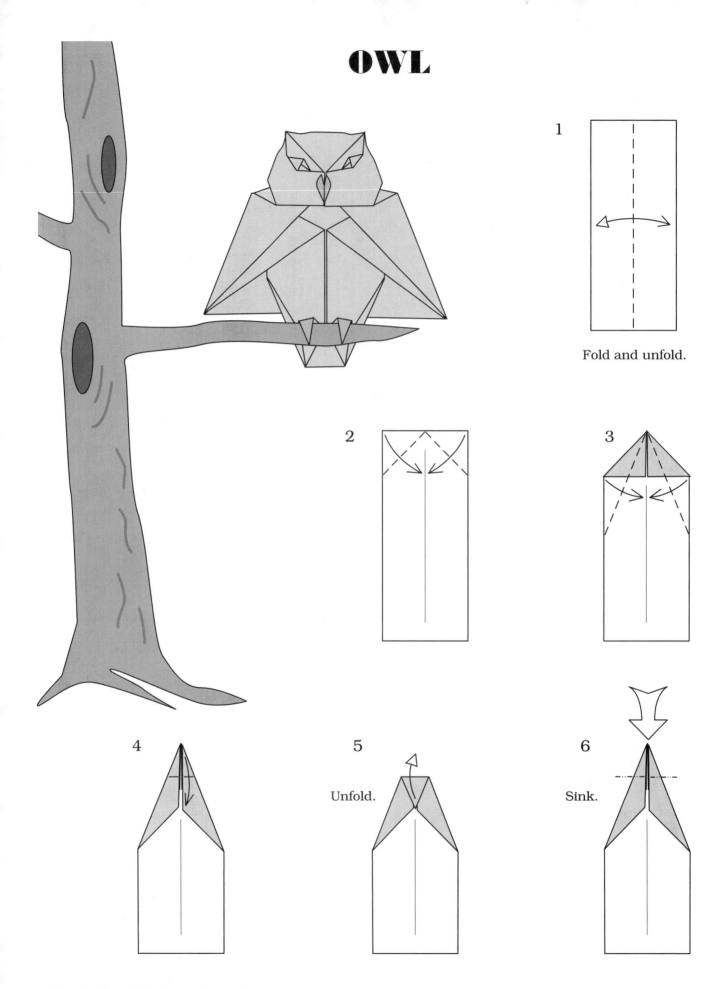

1 Fold and unfold.

2

3

4

5 Unfold.

6 Sink.

7

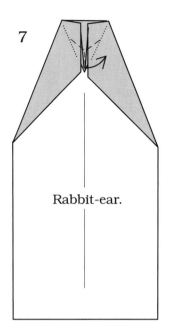

Rabbit-ear.

8

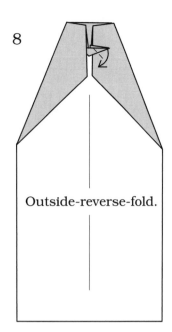

Outside-reverse-fold.

9

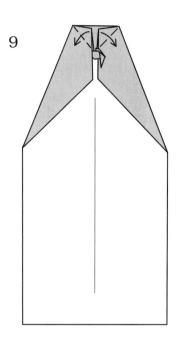

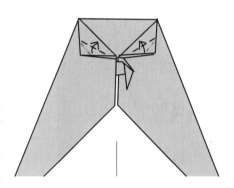

Squash folds.

11

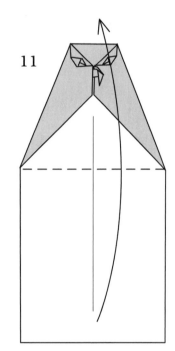

12

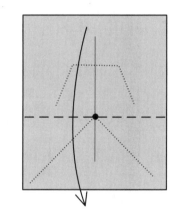

13

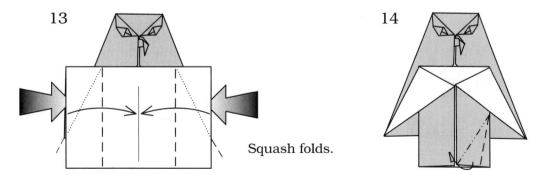

Squash folds.

14

Fold to a point at
the leg but in the
middle at the tail.

15

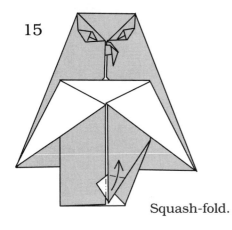

Squash-fold.

16

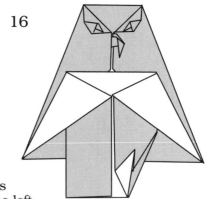

Repeat steps
14–15 on the left.

17

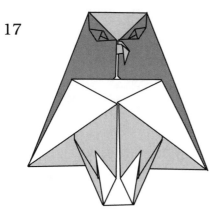

Bring the darker
paper to the front.

18

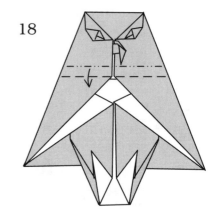

19

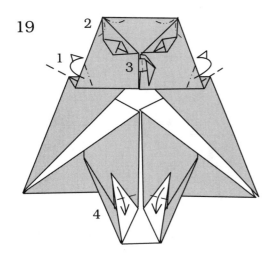

20

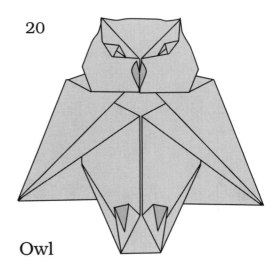

Owl

PARROT

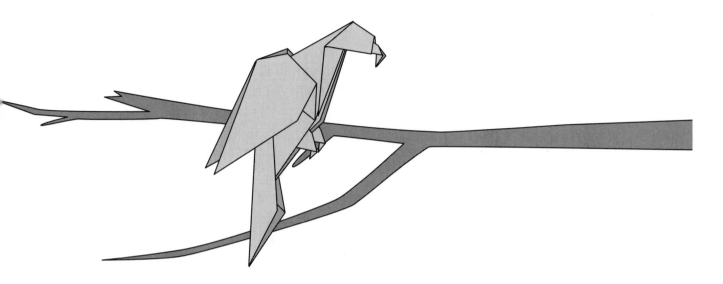

1

2

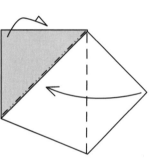

3

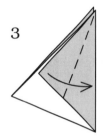

Repeat behind.

4

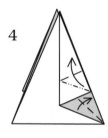

Squash-fold.
Repeat behind.

5

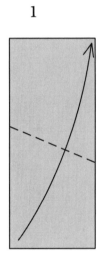

Unfold.

6

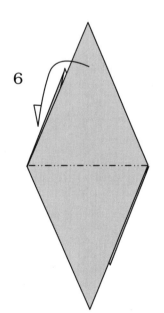

7

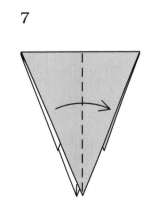

Fold and unfold.

8

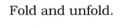

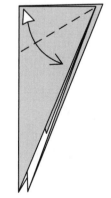

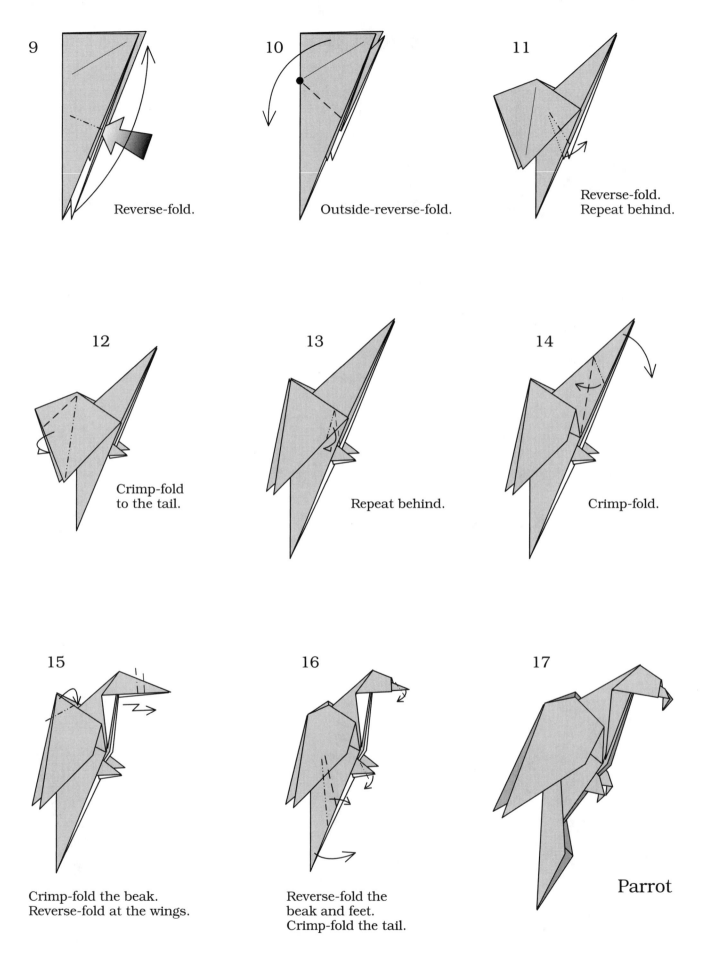

9 Reverse-fold.

10 Outside-reverse-fold.

11 Reverse-fold.
Repeat behind.

12 Crimp-fold
to the tail.

13 Repeat behind.

14 Crimp-fold.

15 Crimp-fold the beak.
Reverse-fold at the wings.

16 Reverse-fold the
beak and feet.
Crimp-fold the tail.

17 Parrot

TOUCAN

1

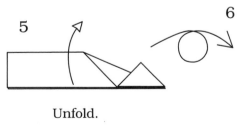

2

3

4

5

Unfold.

6

7

Unfold.

8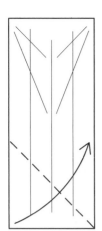

9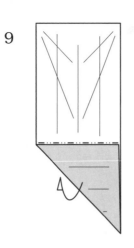

10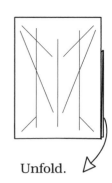

Fold and unfold.

11

Unfold.

12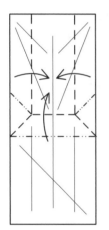

Collapse along
the creases.

13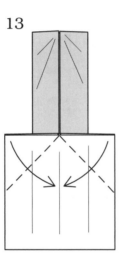

14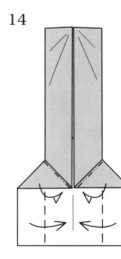

Squash folds.

15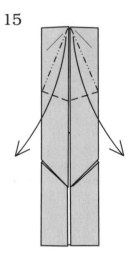

Open.

16

17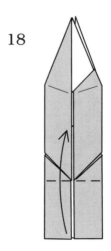

Reverse-fold.

18

19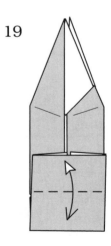

Fold and unfold.

20

21

Squash folds.

22

Bring the wings
to the front.

23

24

Outside-reverse-fold.

25

This is not a symmetric
outside reverse fold.

26

1

2

1. Make a very thin crimp fold.
2. Crimp-fold to form the feet.

27

1

2

3

1. Crimp the beaks
   and separate them.
2. Repeat behind.
3. Shape the feet, repeat behind.

28

Toucan

PENGUIN

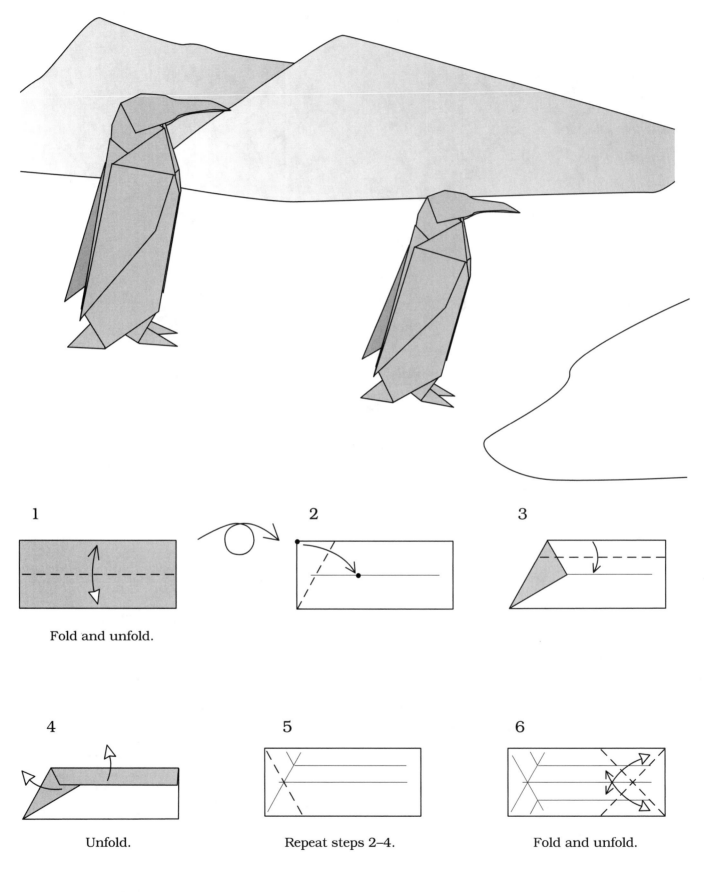

1

Fold and unfold.

2

3

4

Unfold.

5

Repeat steps 2–4.

6

Fold and unfold.

7

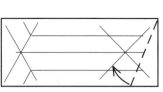

8

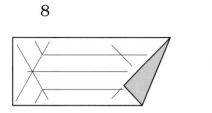

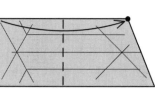

9

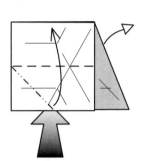

10

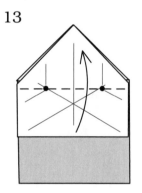

Unfold from behind.
Squash-fold and rotate.

11

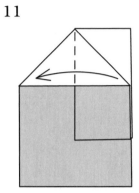

12

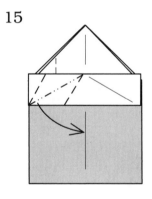

Repeat steps 10–11
on the right.

13

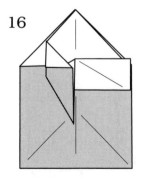

14

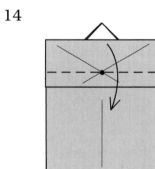

15

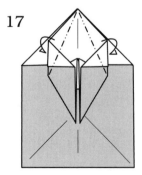

16

Repeat step 15
on the right.

17

18

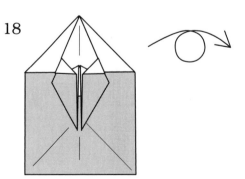

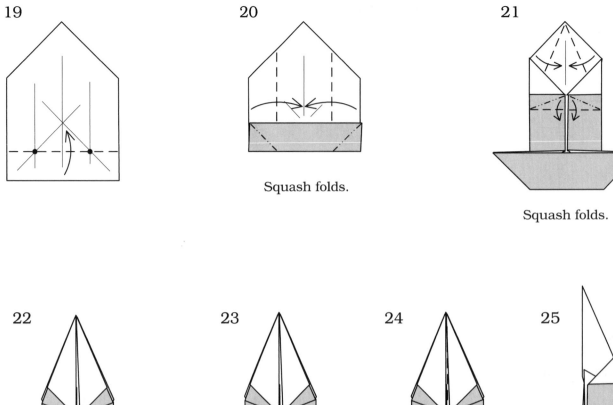

19

20

Squash folds.

21

Squash folds.

22

23

24

25

Rabbit-ear.
Repeat behind.

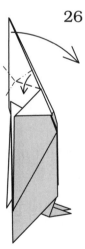

26

This is similar
to a crimp fold.

27

1. Crimp-fold.
2. Repeat behind.
3. Thin and curve the beak.

28

Penguin

SPARROW

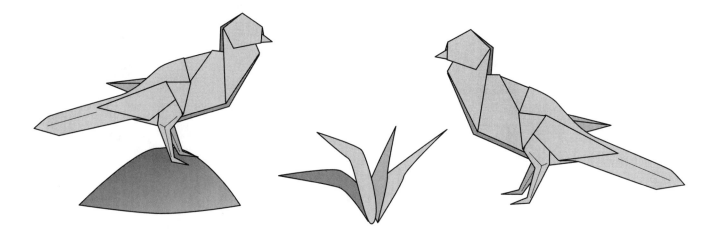

1

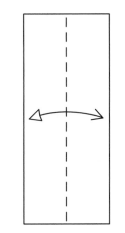

Fold and unfold.

2

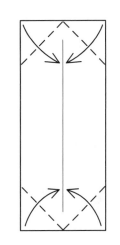

3

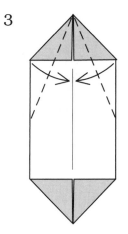

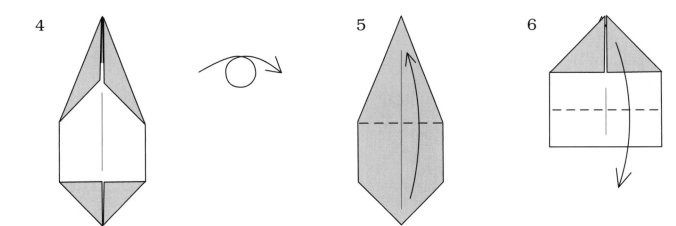

7

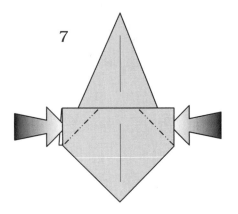

Reverse folds.

8

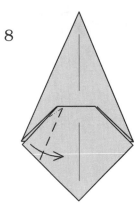

Spread-squash-fold.

9

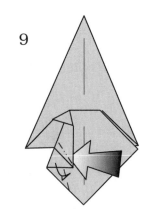

Reverse-fold.

10

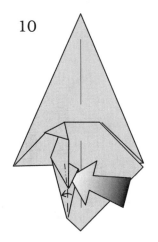

Reverse-fold.

11

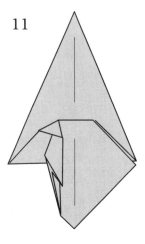

Repeat steps 8–10
on the right.

12

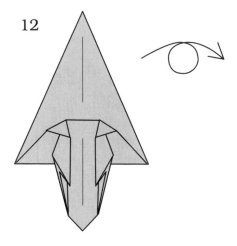

13

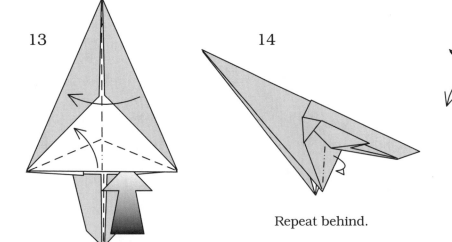

14

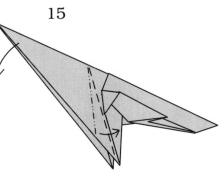

Repeat behind.

15

Crimp-fold.

16

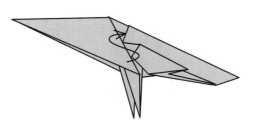

Tuck inside. Repeat behind.

17

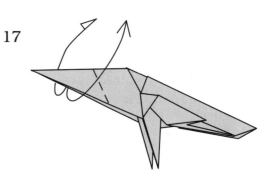

Outside-reverse-fold.

18

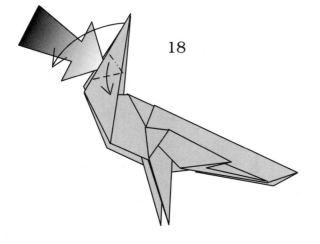

Open the head.

19

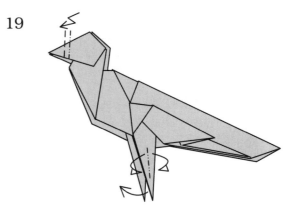

Crimp-fold the beak. Repeat behind for the legs.

20

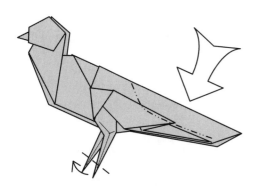

Spread and shape the tail.

21

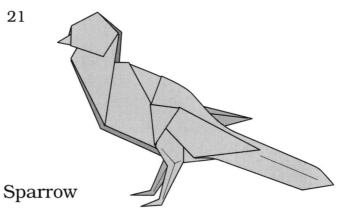

Sparrow

CRANE

1

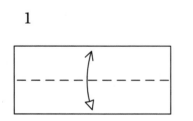

Fold and unfold.

2

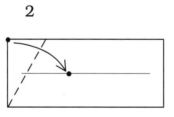

3

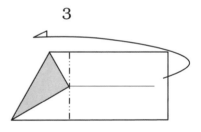

4

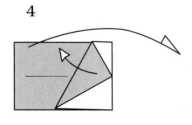

Unfold.

5

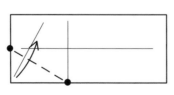

6

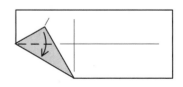

7

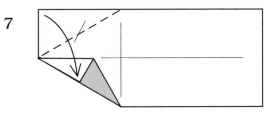

8

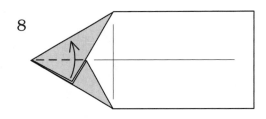

9

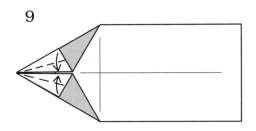

10

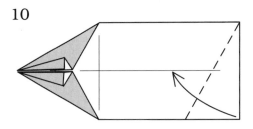

11

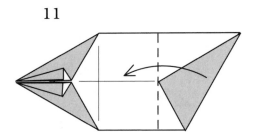

12

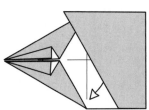

Unfold.

13

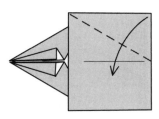

14

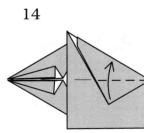

15

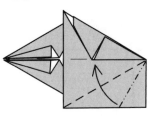

16

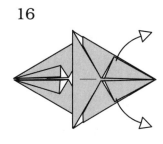

Unfold.

Crane 45

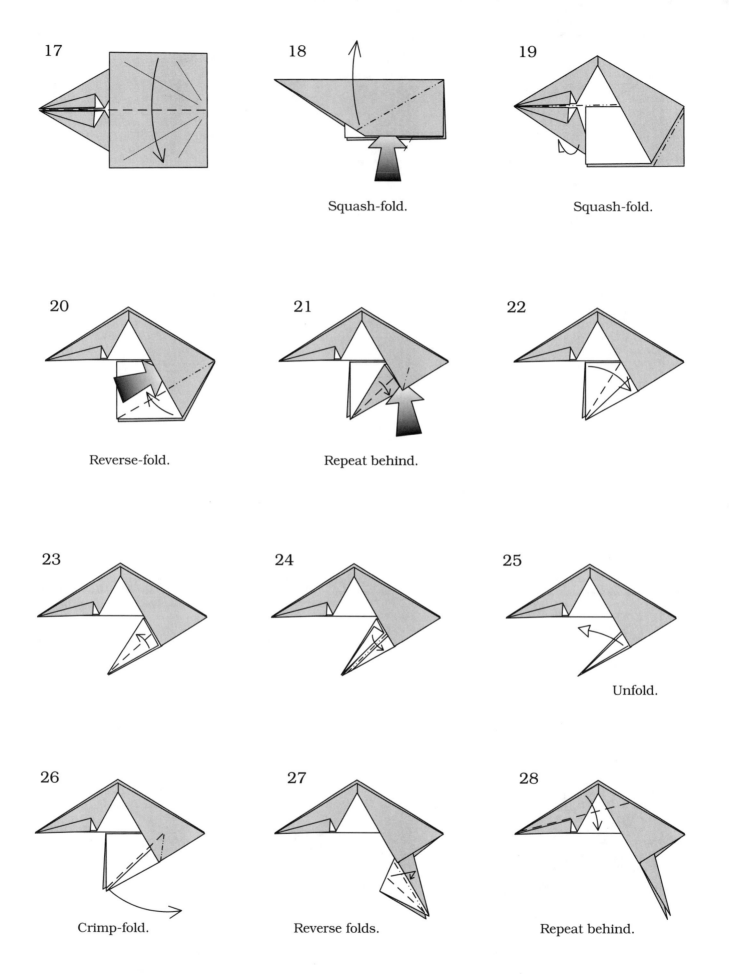

17

18

Squash-fold.

19

Squash-fold.

20

Reverse-fold.

21

Repeat behind.

22

23

24

25

Unfold.

26

Crimp-fold.

27

Reverse folds.

28

Repeat behind.

29

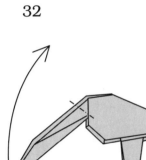

Repeat behind.

30

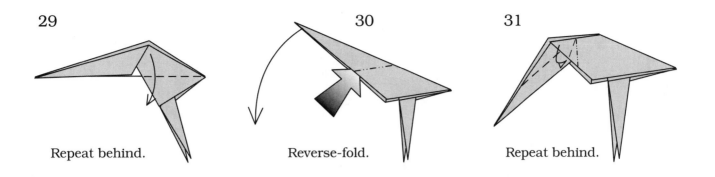

Reverse-fold.

31

Repeat behind.

32

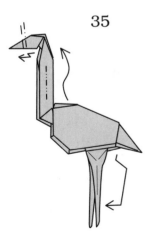

Reverse-fold.

33

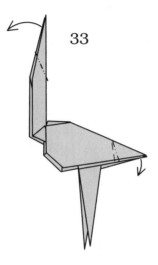

Reverse-fold the head
and crimp-fold the tail.

34

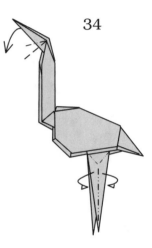

Open the head. Thin the
leg and repeat behind.

35

Crimp-fold the beak.
Shape the legs and
neck. Repeat behind.

36

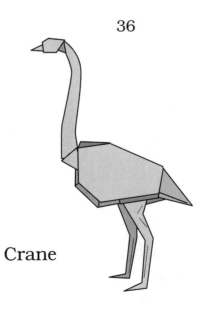

Crane

ROOSTER

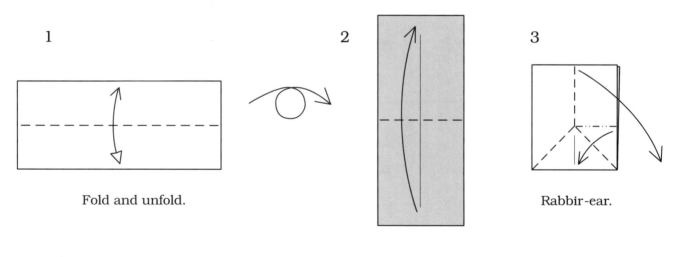

1

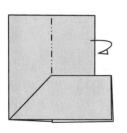

Fold and unfold.

2

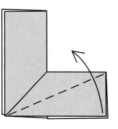

3

Rabbir-ear.

4

5

Repeat behind.

6

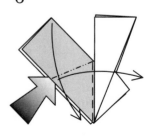

Squash-fold.

7

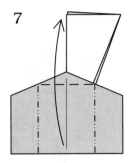

Petal-fold.

8

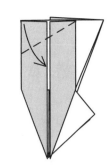

9

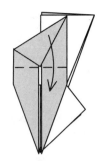

10

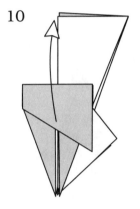

Unfold.

11

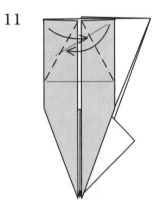

12

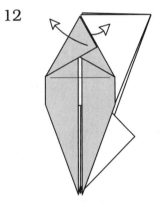

Unfold.

13

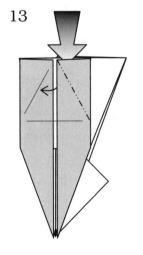

Reverse-fold.

14

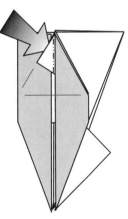

Reverse-fold.

15

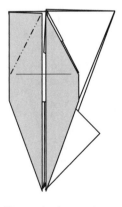

Repeat steps
13–14 on the left.

16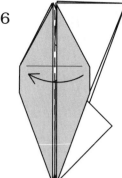

17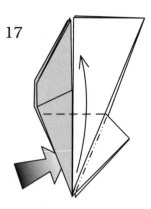

Squash-fold.

18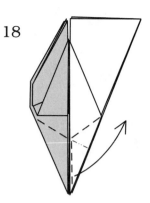

Rabbit-ear.

19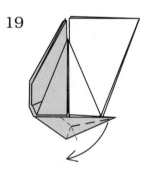

Rabbit-ear.

20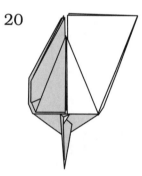

Repeat steps
18–19 above.

21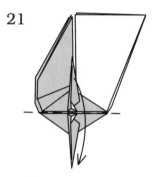

22

Repeat behind.

23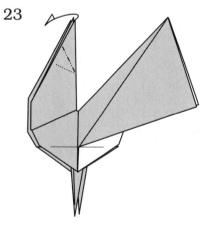

Simple mountain-fold,
repeat behind.

24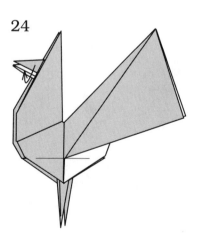

Tuck one inside
the other.

25

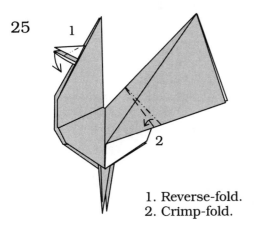

1. Reverse-fold.
2. Crimp-fold.

26

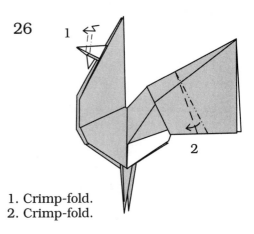

1. Crimp-fold.
2. Crimp-fold.

27

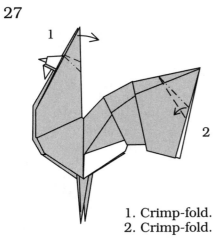

1. Crimp-fold.
2. Crimp-fold.

28

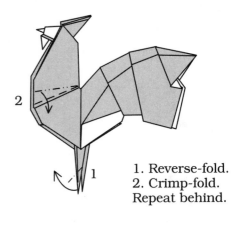

1. Reverse-fold.
2. Crimp-fold.
Repeat behind.

29

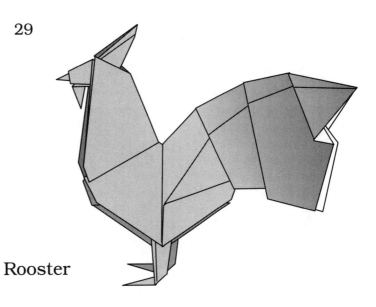

Rooster

SNAKE

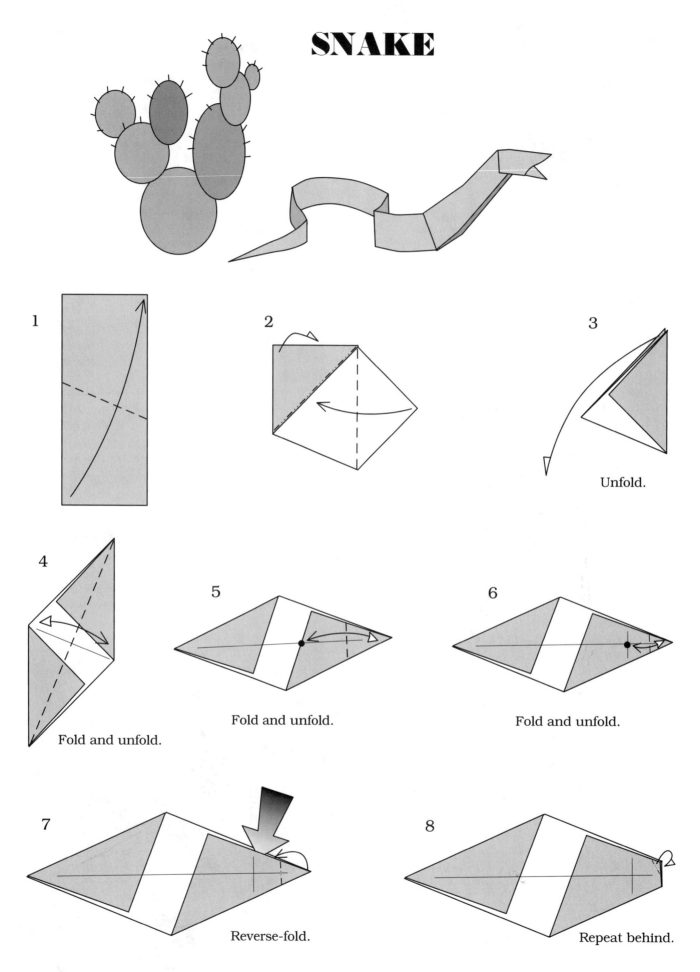

1

2

3

Unfold.

4

Fold and unfold.

5

Fold and unfold.

6

Fold and unfold.

7

Reverse-fold.

8

Repeat behind.

9

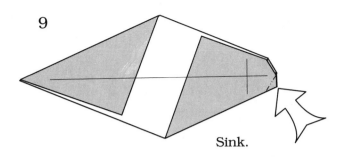

Sink.

10

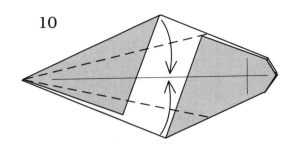

11

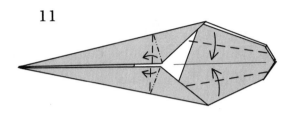

Squash folds.

12

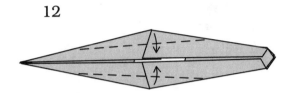

13

14

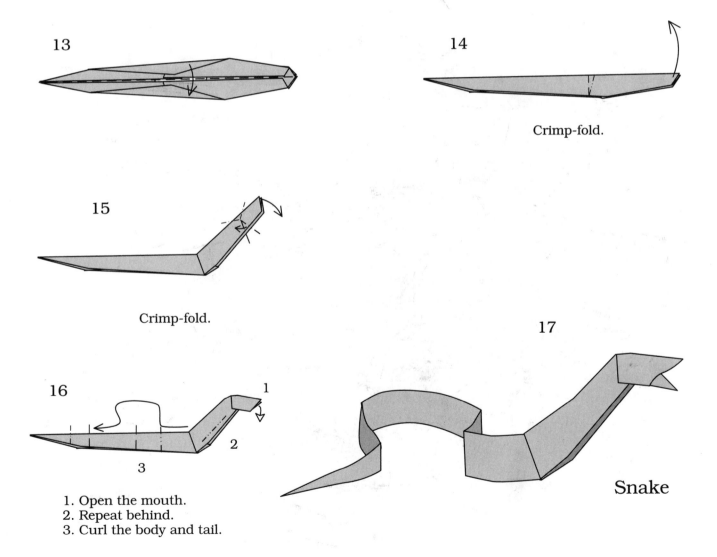

Crimp-fold.

15

Crimp-fold.

16

1
2
3

1. Open the mouth.
2. Repeat behind.
3. Curl the body and tail.

17

Snake

TURTLE

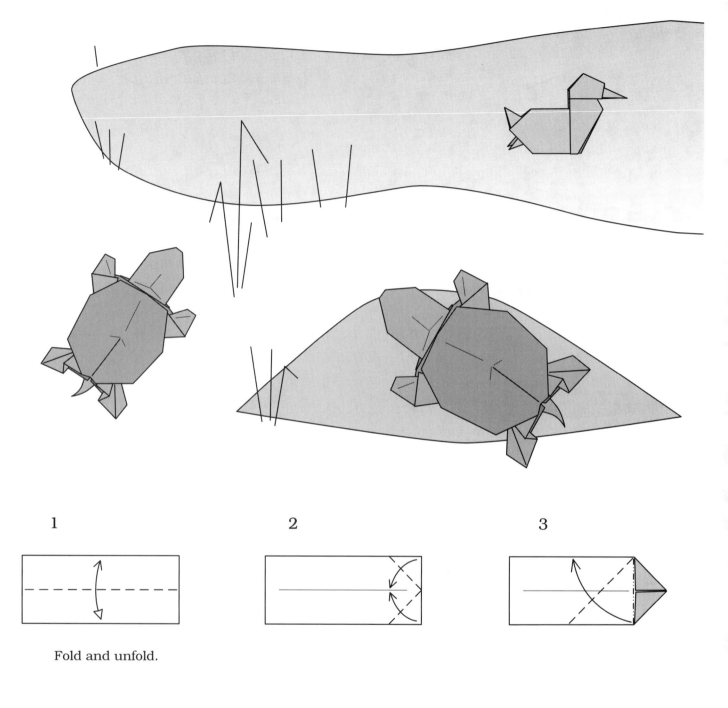

1

Fold and unfold.

2

3

4

Fold and unfold.

5

Unfold.

6

7

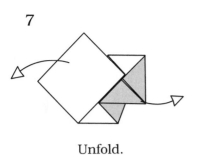

Unfold.

8

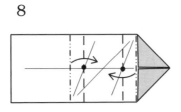

9

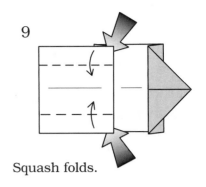

Squash folds.

10

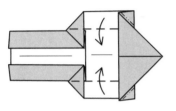

Squash folds.

11

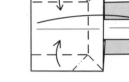

Pull out.

12

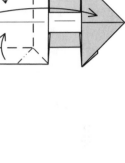

13

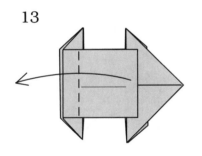

Stretch.

14

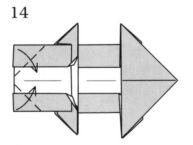

15

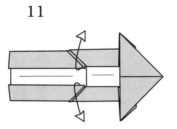

Squash folds.

16

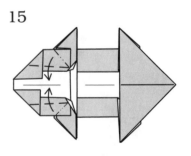

17

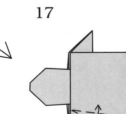

Spread-squash-fold.

18

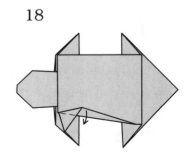

19

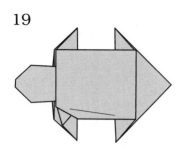

Repeat steps 17-18 on
the three other corners.

20

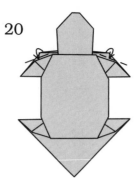

21

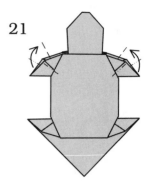

Squash folds.

22

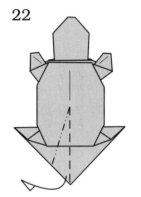

23

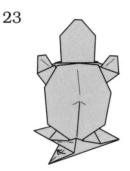

24

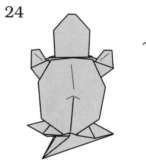

25

Rabbit-ear.

26

27

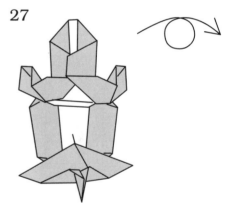

28

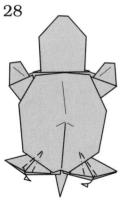

Squash folds.

29

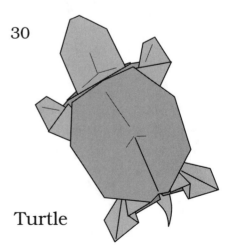

30

Turtle

APATOSAURUS

1

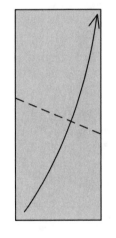

2

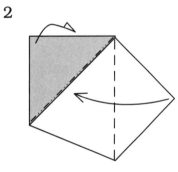

3

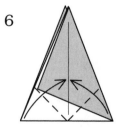

Unfold.

4

Fold and unfold.

5

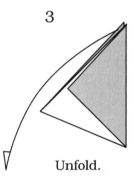

6

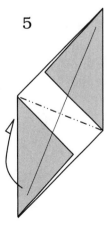

7

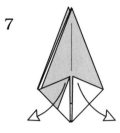

Unfold.

8

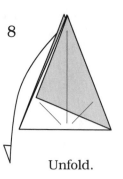

Unfold.

9

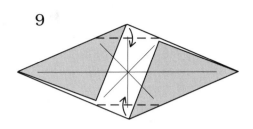

10

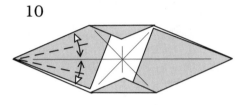

Fold to the center
and unfold.

11

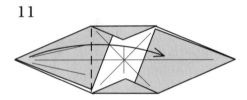

12

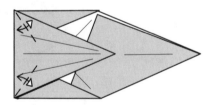

Fold and unfold.

13

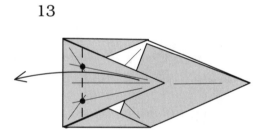

14

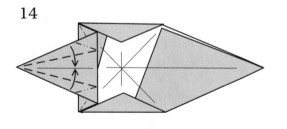

Squash folds.

15

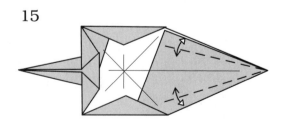

Fold at an angle of
one-third and unfold.

16

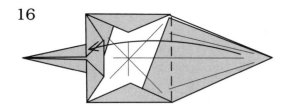

17

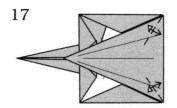

Repeat steps 12–14
on the right.

18

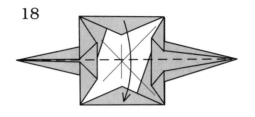

19

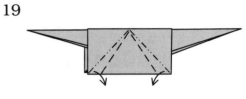

Crimp folds.

20

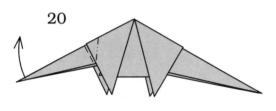

Crimp-fold.

21

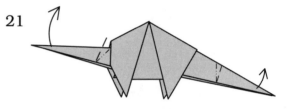

Crimp folds.

22

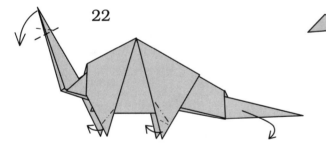

Squash-fold the head, reverse-fold
the front legs, crimp-fold the hind
legs, and curl the tail.

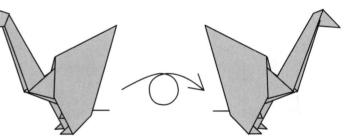

Note that the head is different on each side.

23

Apatosaurus

TRICERATOPS

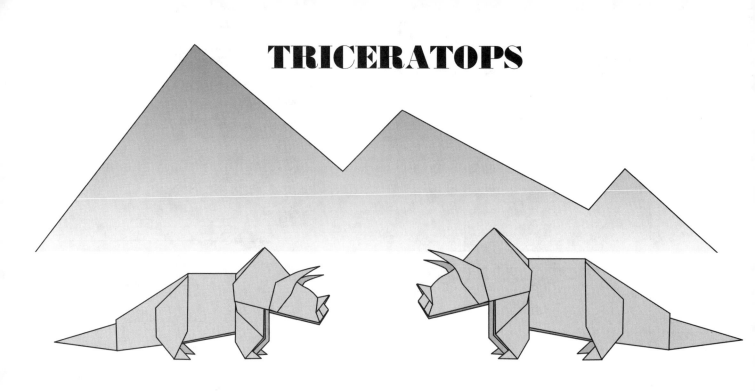

1

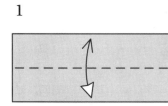

Fold and unfold.

2

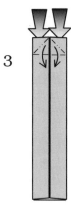

3

Squash folds.

4

Rabbit-ear.

5

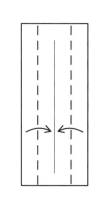

Repeat step 4
on the right.

6

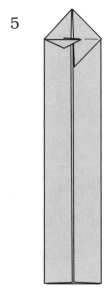

7

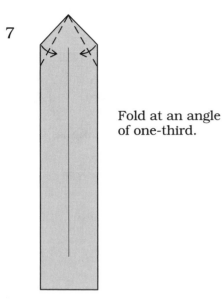

Fold at an angle
of one-third.

8

9

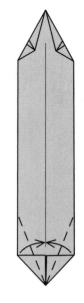

10

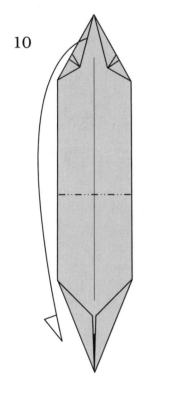

11

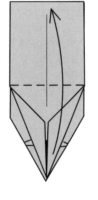

Repeat behind.

12

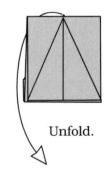

Unfold.

13

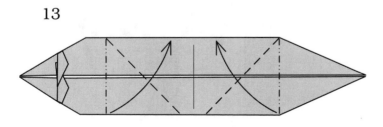

14

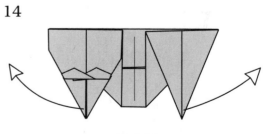

Unfold.

15

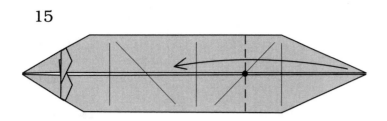

16

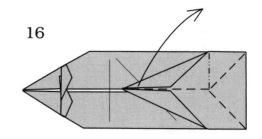

Rabbit-ear.

17

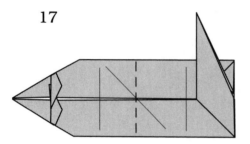

Repeat steps 15–16
on the left.

18

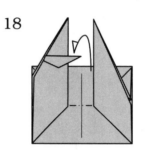

19

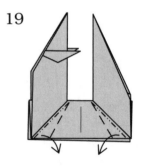

Crimp folds.

20

21

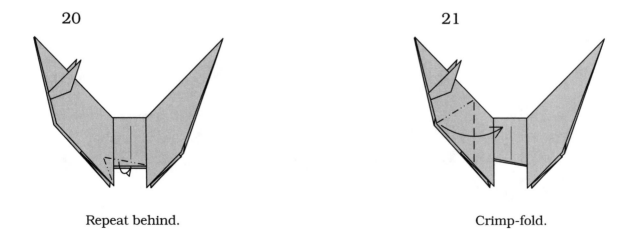

Repeat behind.

Crimp-fold.

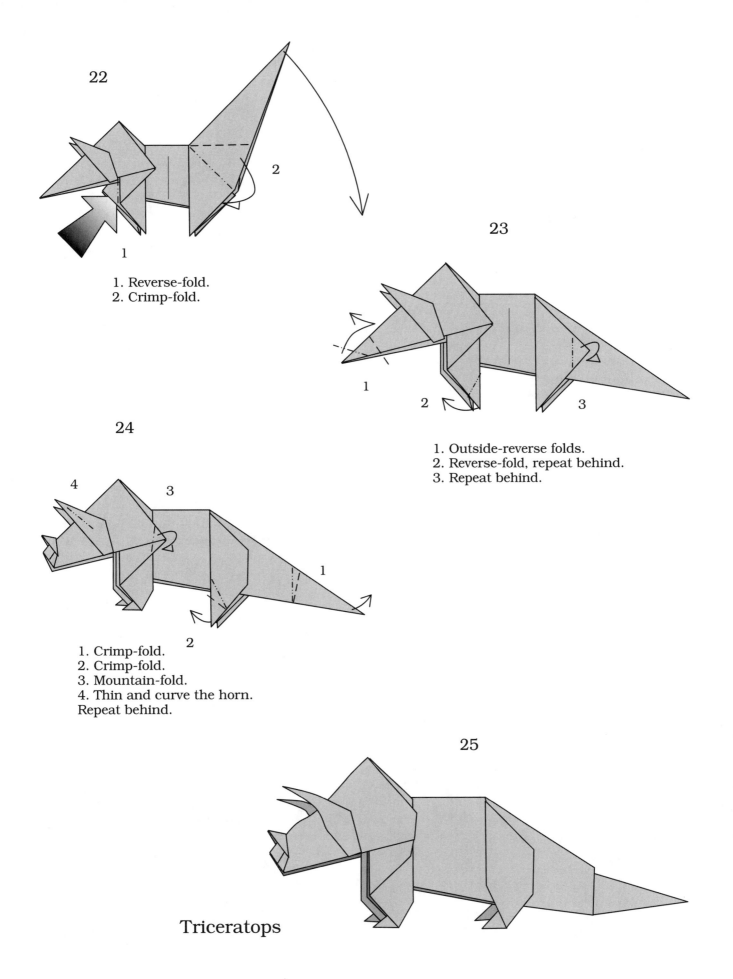

22

1. Reverse-fold.
2. Crimp-fold.

23

1. Outside-reverse folds.
2. Reverse-fold, repeat behind.
3. Repeat behind.

24

1. Crimp-fold.
2. Crimp-fold.
3. Mountain-fold.
4. Thin and curve the horn.
Repeat behind.

25

Triceratops

PIG

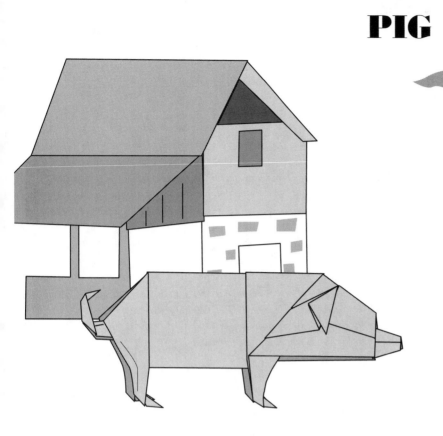

1

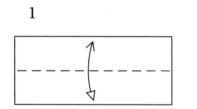

Fold and unfold.

2

3

Unfold.

4

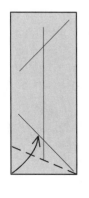

5

6

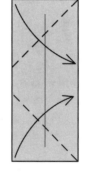

7

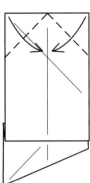

8

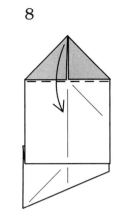

9

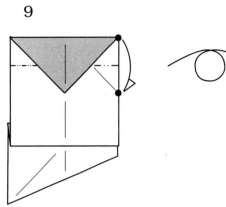

10

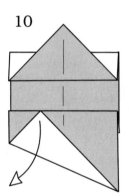

Unfold. Turn
over and rotate.

11

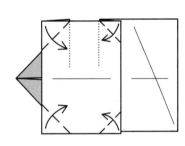

12

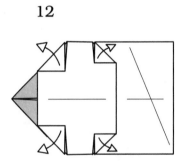

Unfold.

13

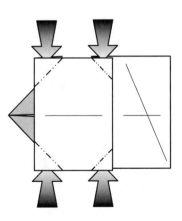

Reverse folds.

14

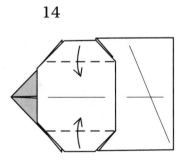

15

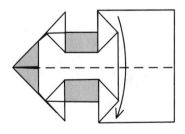

16

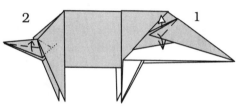

Repeat behind.

17

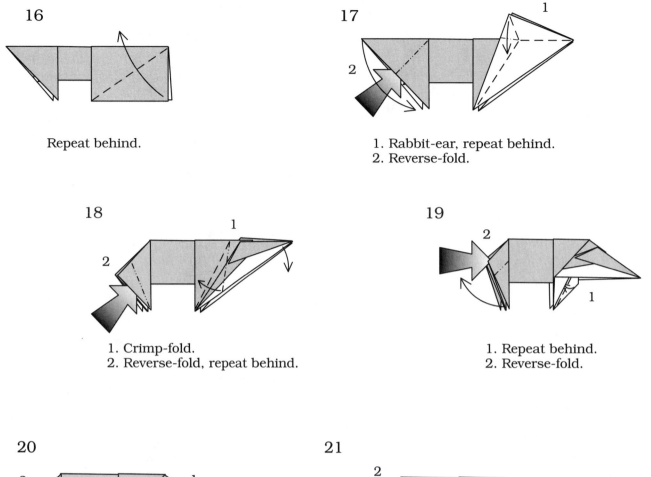

1. Rabbit-ear, repeat behind.
2. Reverse-fold.

18

1. Crimp-fold.
2. Reverse-fold, repeat behind.

19

1. Repeat behind.
2. Reverse-fold.

20

1. Open the ear.
2. Reverse-fold.
Repeat behind.

21

1. Crimp-fold.
2. Reverse folds.
3. Reverse-folds.
Repeat behind.

22

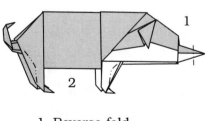

1. Reverse-fold.
2. Shape the legs.
Repeat behind.

23

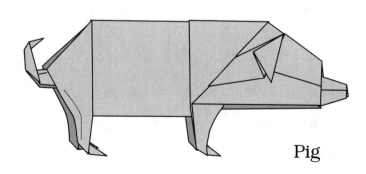
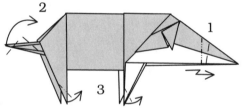

Pig

SITTING CAT

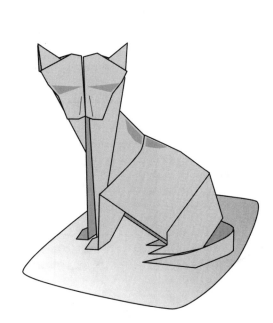

1

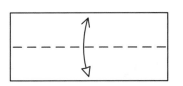

Fold and unfold.

2

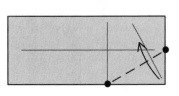

3

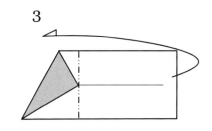

4

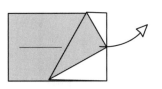

Unfold.

5

6

Rabbit-ear.

7

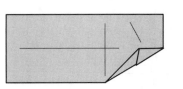

Repeat steps 5–6 on the top.

8

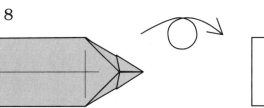

9

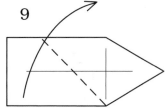

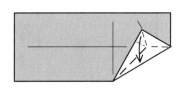

10

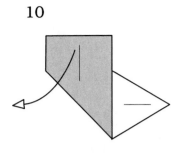

Unfold.

11

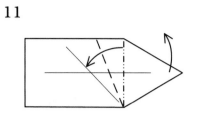

12

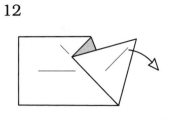

Unfold.

13

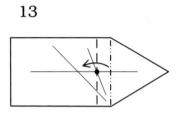

14

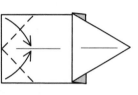

15

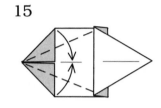

16

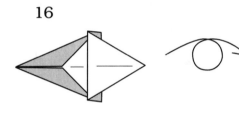

17

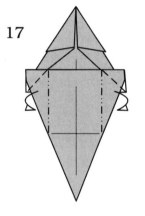

18

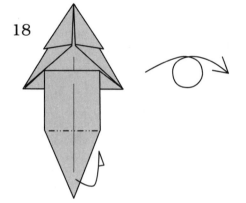

19

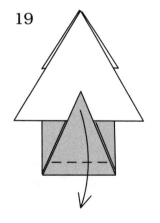

20

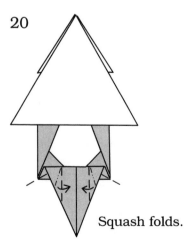

Squash folds.

21

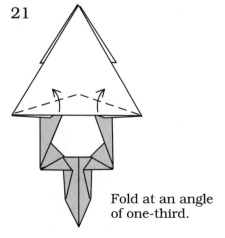

Fold at an angle
of one-third.

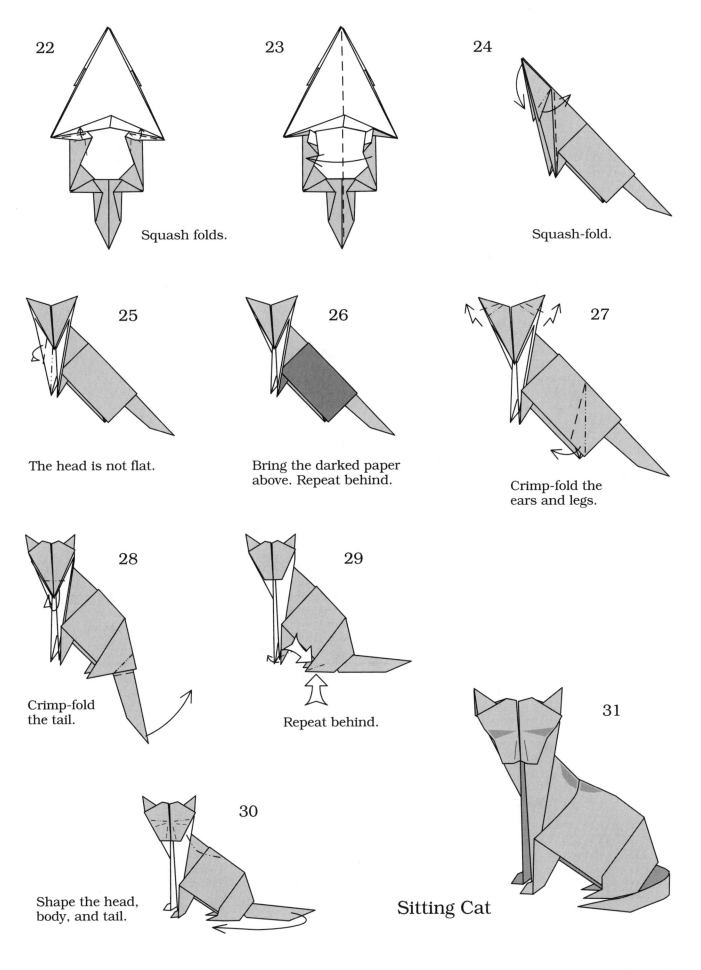

22

23

24
Squash folds.

Squash-fold.

25
The head is not flat.

26
Bring the darked paper above. Repeat behind.

27
Crimp-fold the ears and legs.

28
Crimp-fold the tail.

29
Repeat behind.

30
Shape the head, body, and tail.

31
Sitting Cat

DOG

1

Fold and unfold.

2

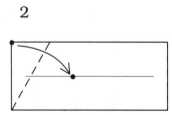

3

4

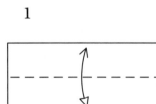

Unfold.

5

6

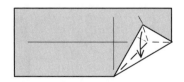

Rabbit-ear.

7

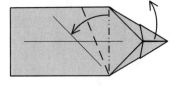

Repeat steps 5–6 on the top.

8

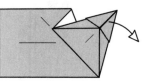

9

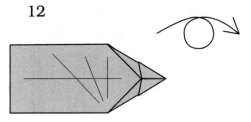

Unfold.

10

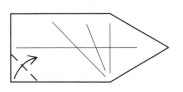

11

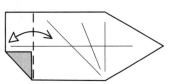

Unfold.

12

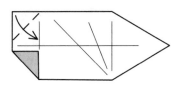

13

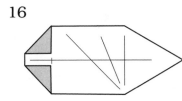

There are no guidelines
for this fold.

14

Fold and unfold.

15

16

17

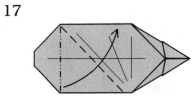

18

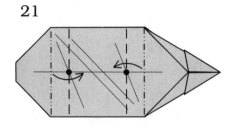

Unfold.

19

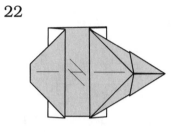

20

Unfold.

21

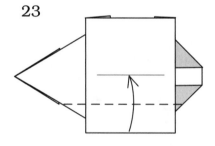

22

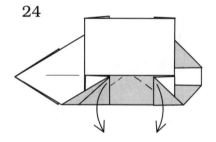

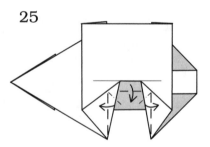

23

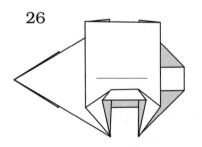

24

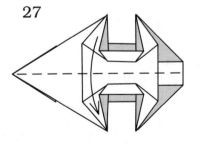

25

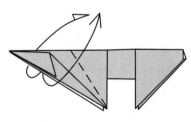

Squash folds.

26

Repeat steps
23–25 above.

27

28

Outside-reverse-fold.

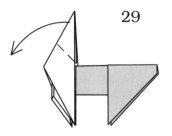

29

Outside-reverse-fold.

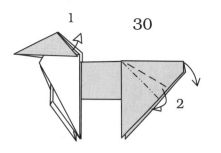

30

1. Pull out, repeat behind.
2. Crimp-fold.

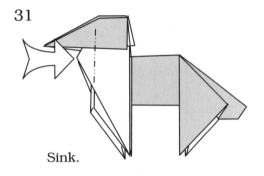

31

Sink.

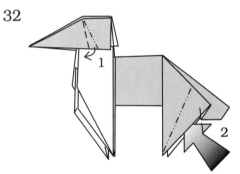

32

Repeat behind.

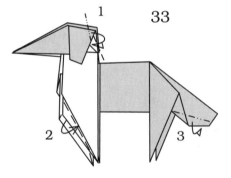

33

1. Reverse-fold.
2. Tuck inside.
3. Mountain-fold.
Repeat behind.

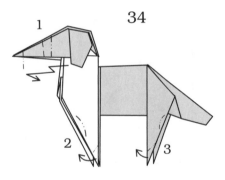

34

Reverse and crimp folds, repeat behind.

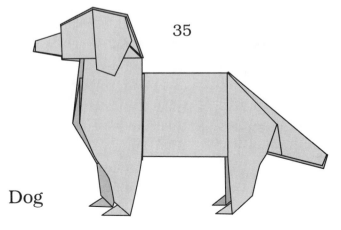

35

Dog

MOUSE

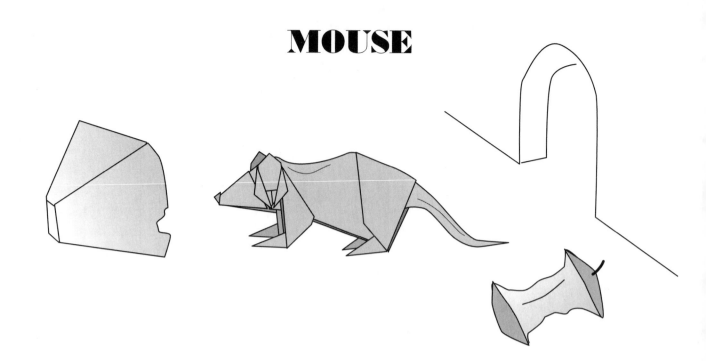

1

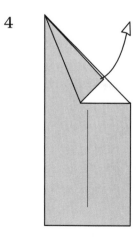

Fold and unfold.

2

3

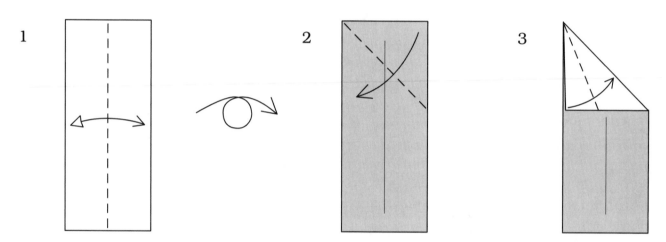

4

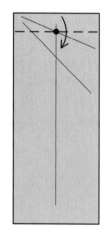

Unfold.

5

6

7

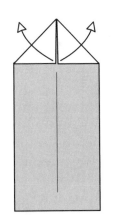

Unfold.

8

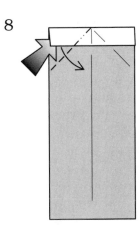

Reverse-fold.

9

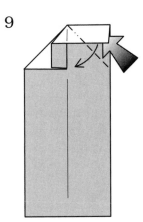

Reverse-fold.

10

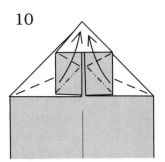

Squash folds.

11

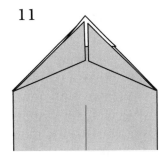

12

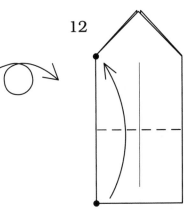

13

Unfold.

14

15

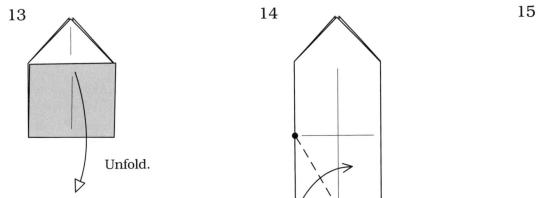

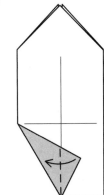

Mouse 75

16

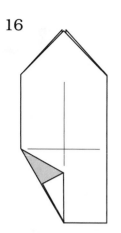

Repeat steps
14–15 on the right.

17

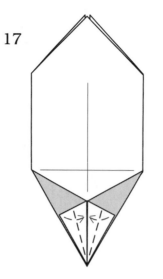

18

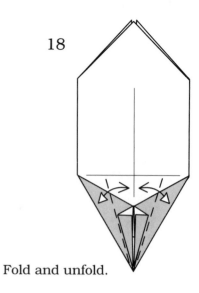

Fold and unfold.

19

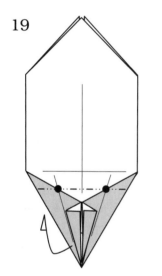

20

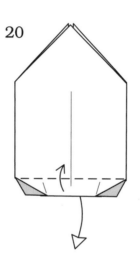

21

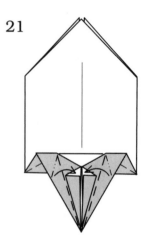

Squash folds.

22 **23** **24**

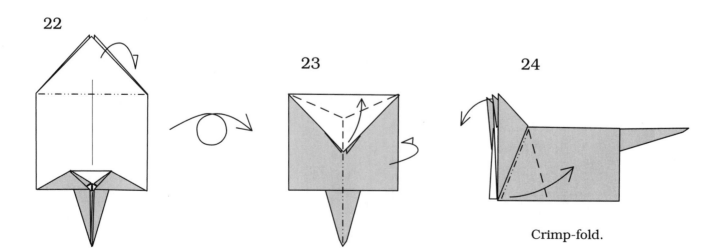

Crimp-fold.

25

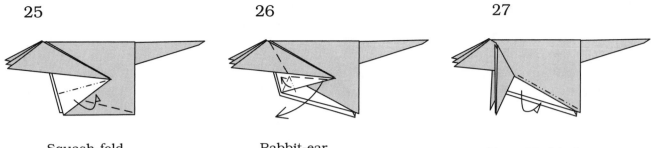

Squash-fold.
Repeat behind.

26

Rabbit-ear.
Repeat behind.

27

Repeat behind.

28

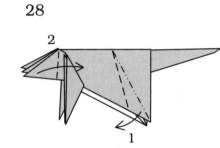

1. Crimp-fold.
2. Repeat behind.

29

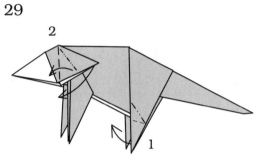

1. Crimp-fold.
2. Squash-fold.
Repeat behind.

30

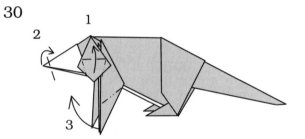

1. Petal-fold the ear.
2. Outside-reverse-fold the nose.
3. Reverse-fold the leg.
Repeat behind.

31

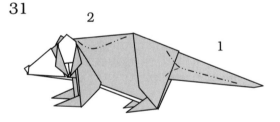

1. Thin and curve the tail.
2. Shape the body.

32

Mouse

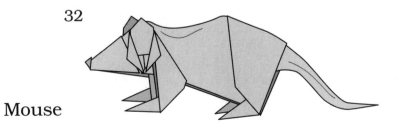

RABBIT

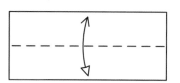

1

Fold and unfold.

2

3

Unfold.

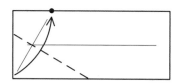

4

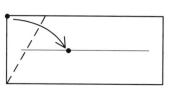

5

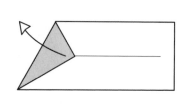

6

Unfold.

7

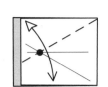

Fold and unfold.

8

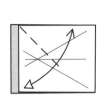

Fold and unfold.

9

Fold and unfold.

10

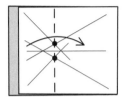

11

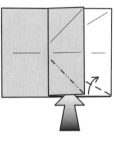

Fold inside.

12

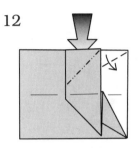

Fold inside.

13

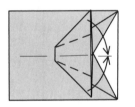

14

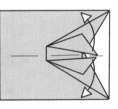

Unfold.

15

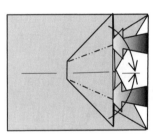

Reverse folds.

16

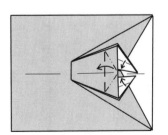

Petal-fold.

17

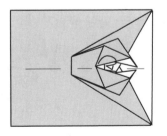

Fold inside.

18

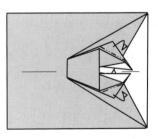

Reverse folds.

19

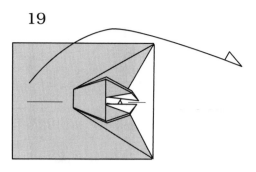

Unfold.

20

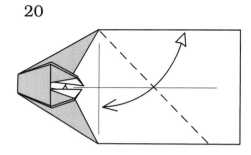

Fold and unfold.

21

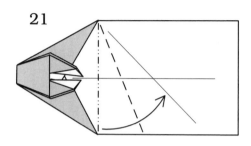

22

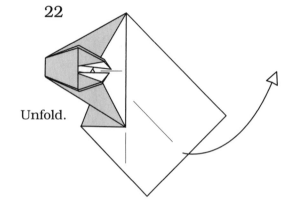

Unfold.

23

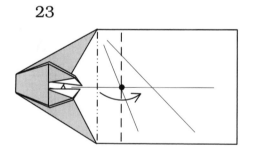

24

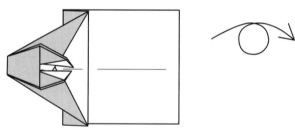

25

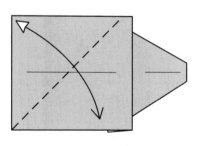

Fold and unfold.

26

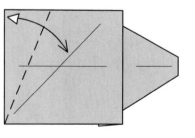

Fold and unfold.

27

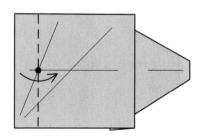

28

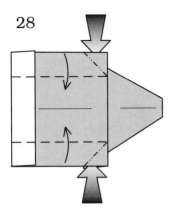

Squash folds.

29

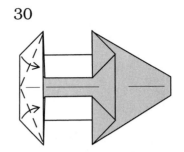

Pull out.

30

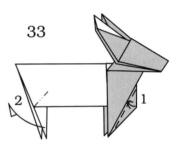

31

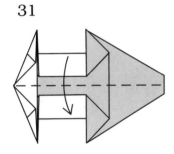

32

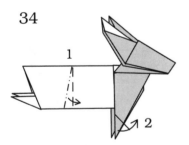

Make two outside reverse folds.

33

2

1

1. Tuck inside.
2. Mountain-fold.
Repeat behind.

34

1

2

1. Crimp-fold.
2. Reverse-fold.
Repeat behind.

36

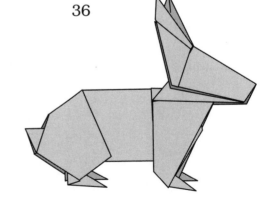

Rabbit

35

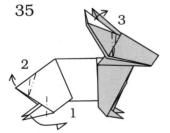

3

2

1

1. Mountain-fold.
2. Crimp-fold.
3. Shape the ears.
Repeat behind.

UNICORN

1

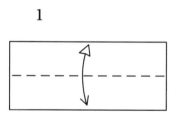

Fold and unfold.

2

Fold the corner to
the center edge.

3

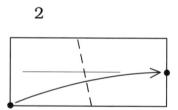

Squash-fold.

4

Center as much
as possible.

5

Unfold.

6

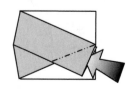

Reverse-fold.

7

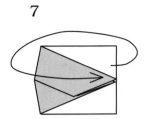

Wrap the paper in back
all the way to the front.

8

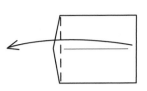

9

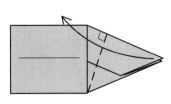

Note the right angle.

10

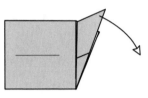

11

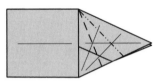

Unfold.

12

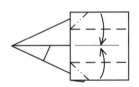

Repeat steps 9–11.

13

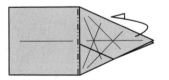

14

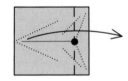

Use the creases from
the hidden triangle
for the land mark.

15

Fold the edges to
the center for these
squash folds.

16

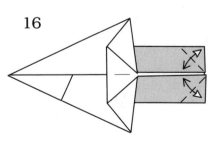

Fold and unfold.

17

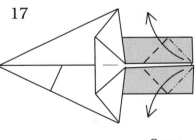

Open.

18

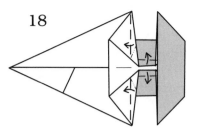

Squash folds.

19

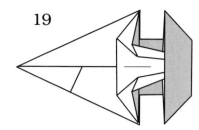

20

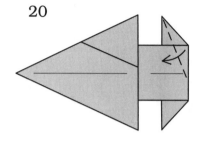

21

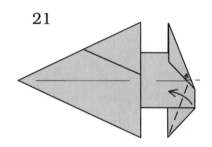

22

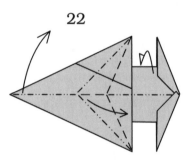

Collapse along the creases.

23

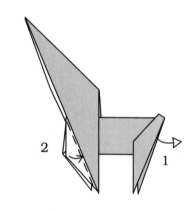

1. Unfold.
2. Tuck, repeat behind.

24

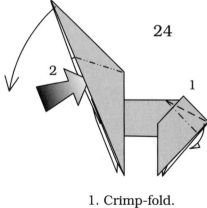

1. Crimp-fold.
2. Reverse-fold.

25

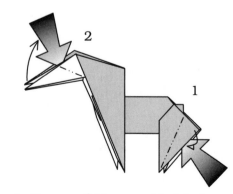

1. Reverse-fold, repeat behind.
2. Reverse-fold.

26

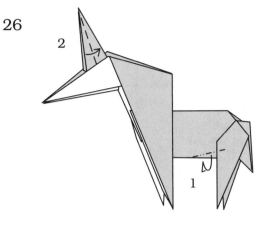

Repeat behind.

27

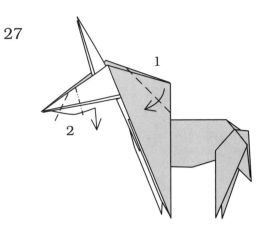

1. Valley-fold the mane.
2. Reverse folds.

28

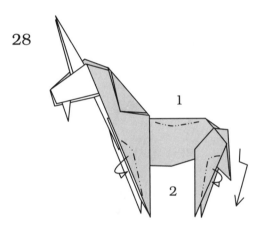

1. Shape the legs, repeat behind.
2. Shape the back.

29

Unicorn

HORSE

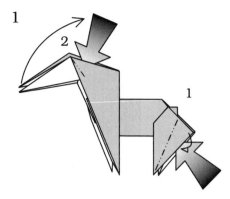

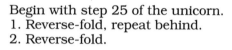

Begin with step 25 of the unicorn.
1. Reverse-fold, repeat behind.
2. Reverse-fold.

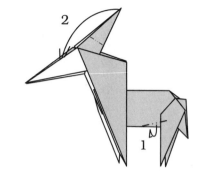

1. Repeat behind.
2. Reverse-fold.

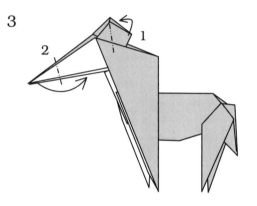

1. Reverse-fold the ears.
2. Reverse-fold.

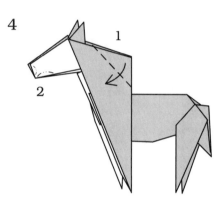

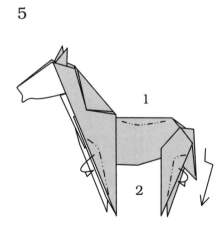

1. Shape the legs, repeat behind.
2. Shape the back.

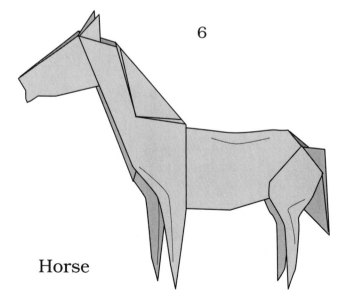

Horse

COW

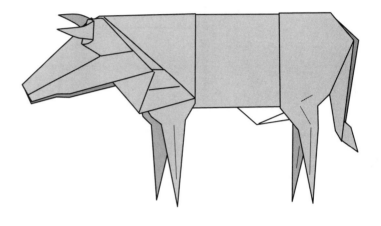

1

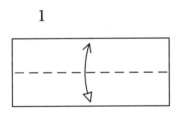

Fold and unfold.

2

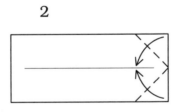

3

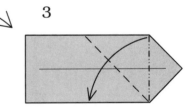

4

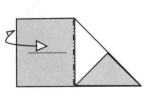

Fold and unfold.

5

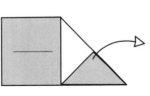

Unfold.

6

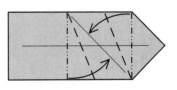

7

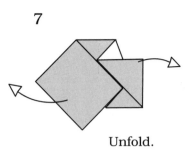

Unfold.

8

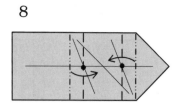

9

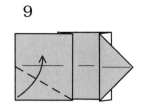

10

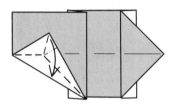

Rabbit-ear.

11

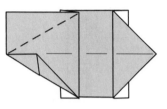

Repeat steps
9–10 above.

12

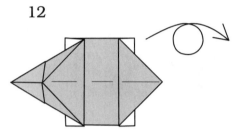

13

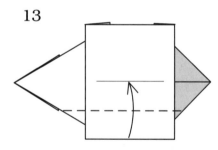

14

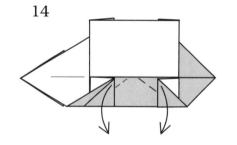

15

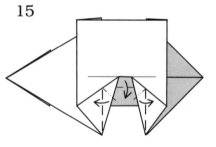

Squash folds.

16

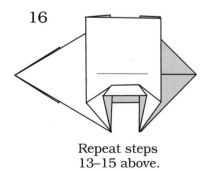

Repeat steps
13–15 above.

17

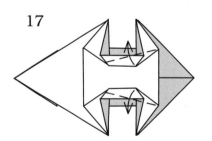

18

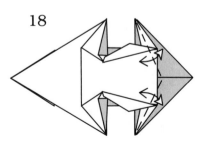

Fold and unfold.

19

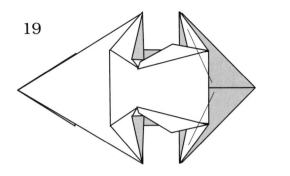

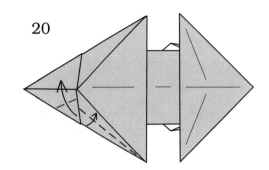

20

Squash-fold.

21

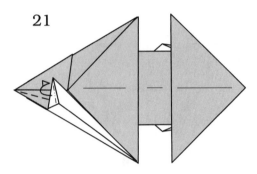

22

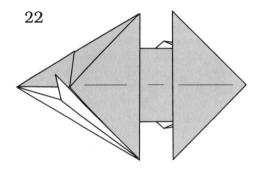

Repeat steps 20–21 above.

23

24

25

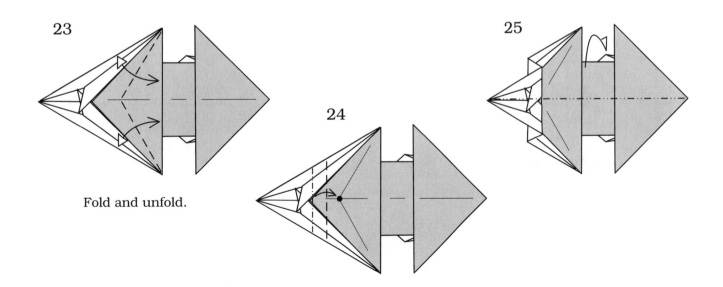

Fold and unfold.

Cow 89

26

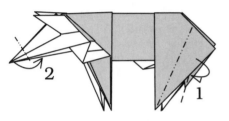

Crimp-fold.

27

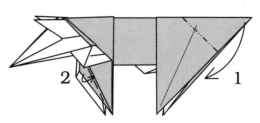

1. Reverse-fold.
2. Tuck inside, repeat behind.

28

1. Reverse-fold. reepat behind.
2. Reverse-fold.

29

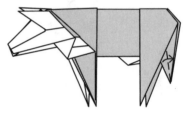

Repeat behind.

30

Repeat behind.

31

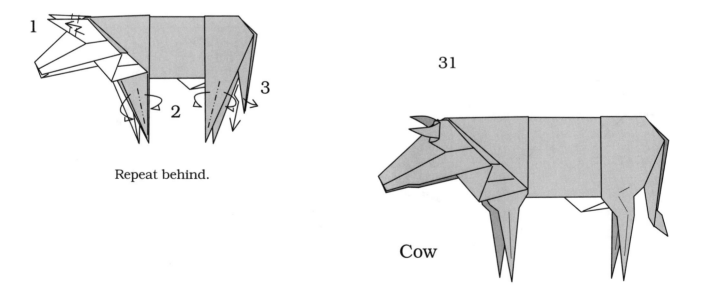

Cow

KANGAROO

1

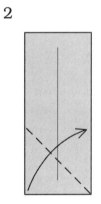

Fold and unfold.

2

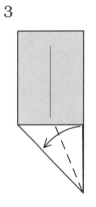

3

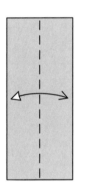

4

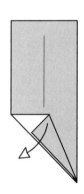

Unfold.

5

6

Unfold.

7

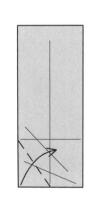

8

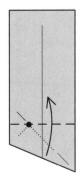

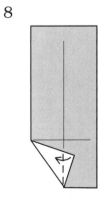

Kangaroo 91

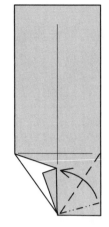

9

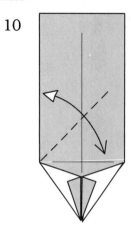

10

Fold and unfold.

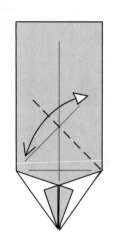

11

Fold and unfold.

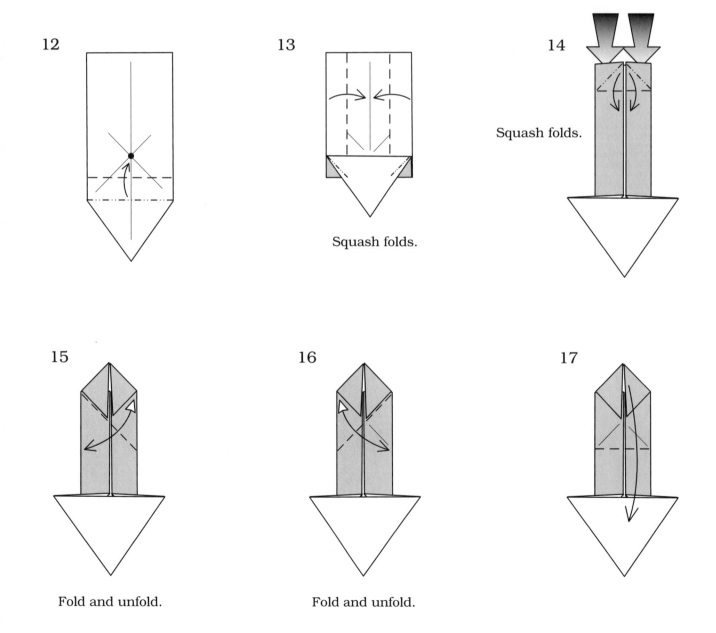

12

13

Squash folds.

14

Squash folds.

15

Fold and unfold.

16

Fold and unfold.

17

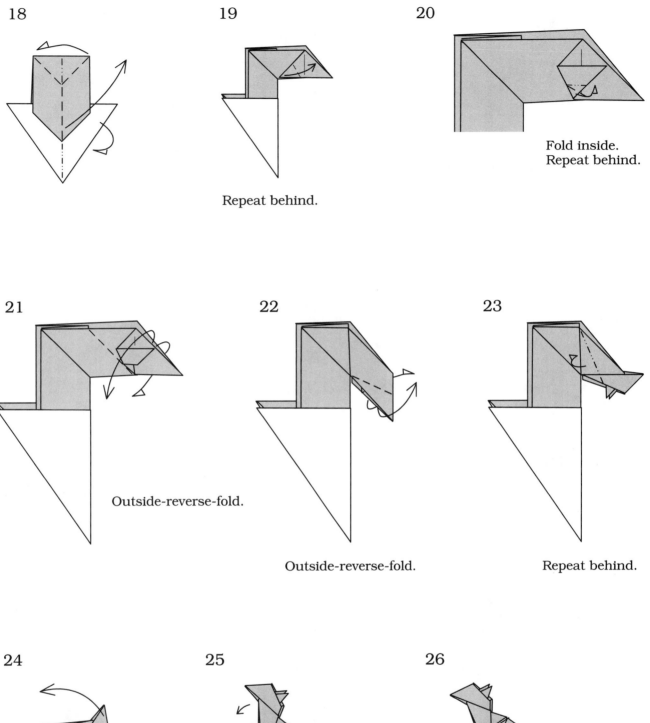

18

19

Repeat behind.

20

Fold inside.
Repeat behind.

21

Outside-reverse-fold.

22

Outside-reverse-fold.

23

Repeat behind.

24

Crimp-fold.

25

Crimp-fold.

26

Reverse-fold.

Kangaroo 93

27

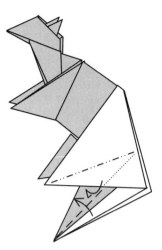

Fold inside.
Repeat behind.

28

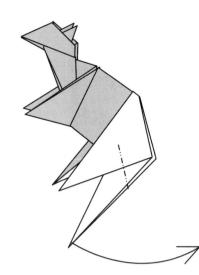

Reverse-fold.

29

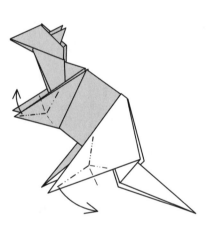

Make the arms and legs
three-dimensional with
rabbit ears. Repeat behind.

30

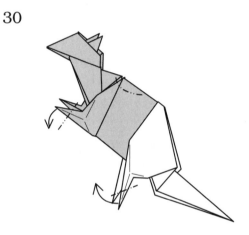

Fold the arms, legs,
and shape the back.
Repeat behind.

31

Kangaroo

ELEPHANT

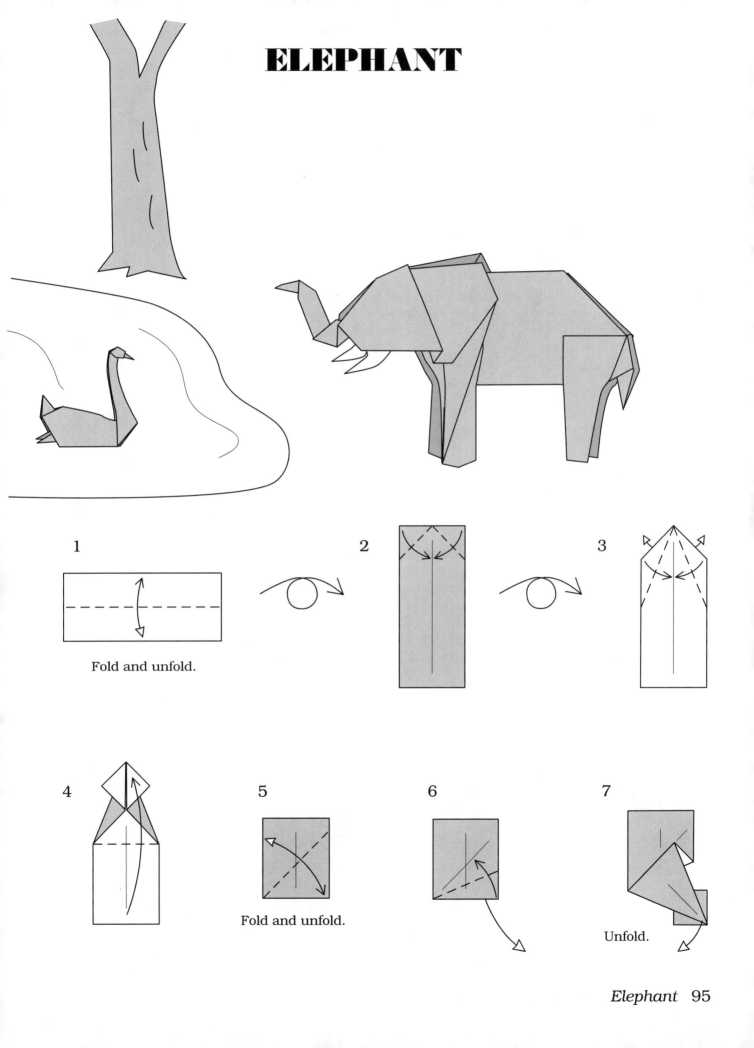

1

Fold and unfold.

2

3

4

5

Fold and unfold.

6

7

Unfold.

8

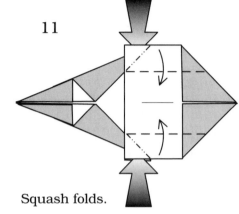

9

10

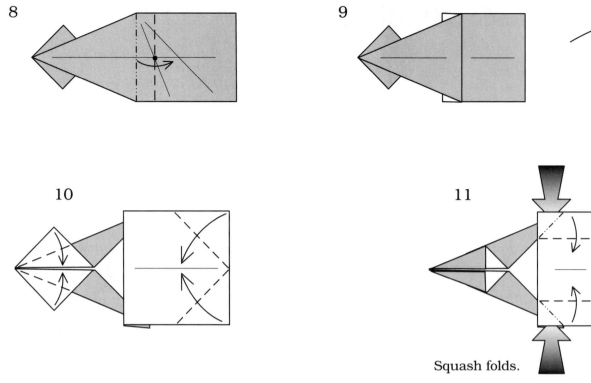

11

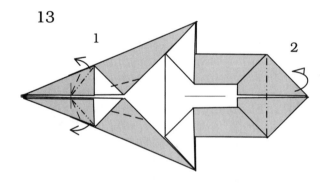

Squash folds.

12

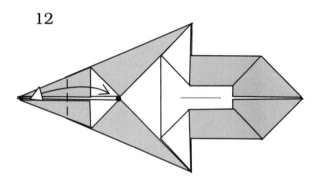

Fold and unfold.

13

1

2

1. Squash folds.
2. Mountain-fold.

14

1

2

1. Squash folds.
2. Pull out the legs.

15

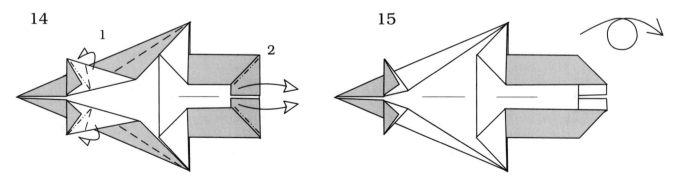

16

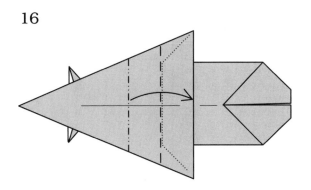

17

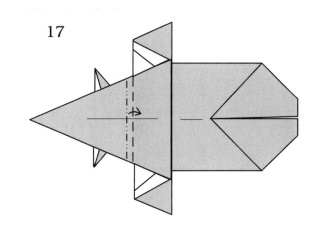

18

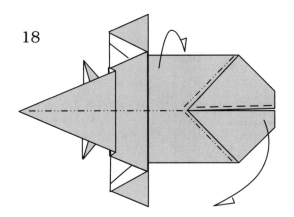

19

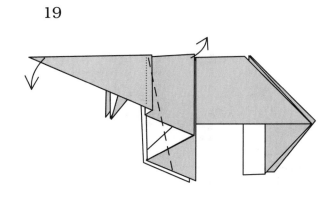

Slide the head.

20

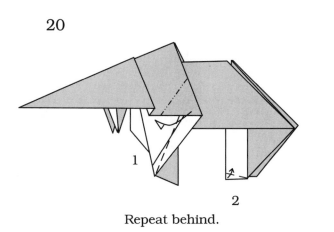

1

2

Repeat behind.

21

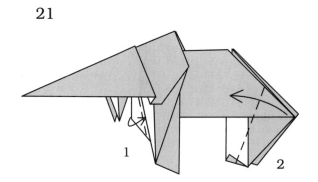

1

2

Repeat behind.

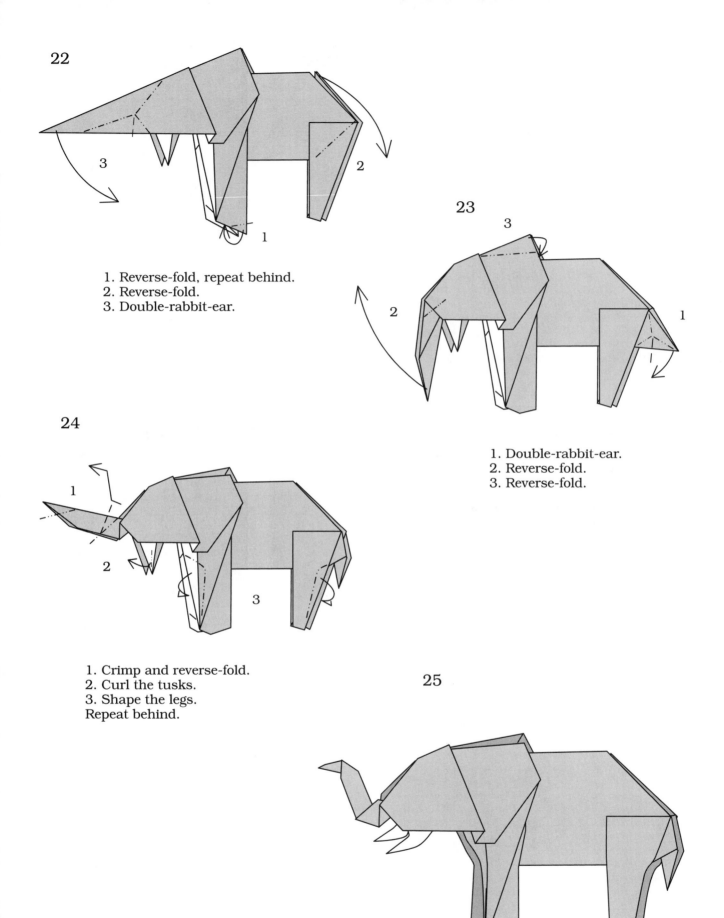

22

1. Reverse-fold, repeat behind.
2. Reverse-fold.
3. Double-rabbit-ear.

23

1. Double-rabbit-ear.
2. Reverse-fold.
3. Reverse-fold.

24

1. Crimp and reverse-fold.
2. Curl the tusks.
3. Shape the legs.
Repeat behind.

25

Elephant

RHINOCEROS

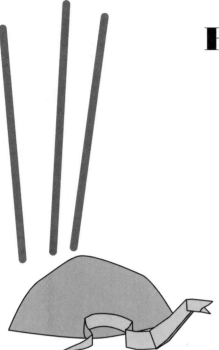

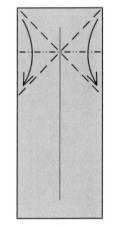

1

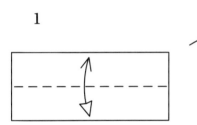

Fold and unfold.

2

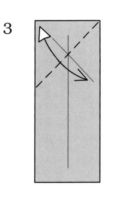

Fold and unfold.

3

Fold and unfold.

4

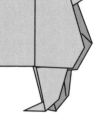

5

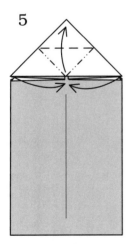

Petal-fold.

6

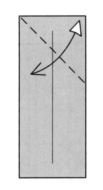

Reverse folds.

7

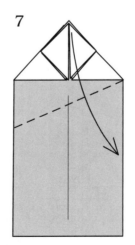

8

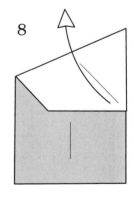

Unfold.

9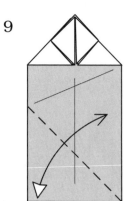

Fold and unfold.

10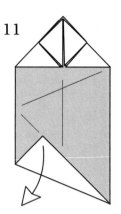

11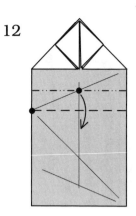

Unfold.

12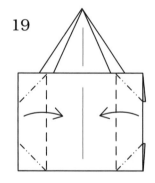

13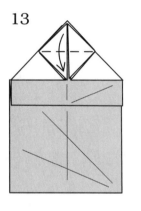

14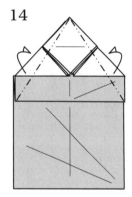

15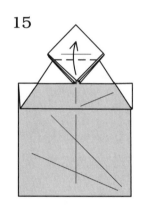

16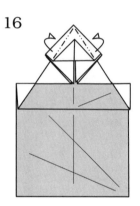

Tuck.

17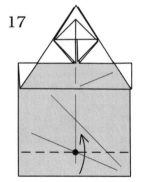

18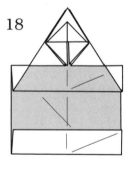

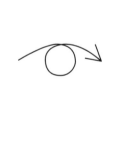

19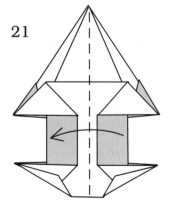

Petal folds.

20

Fold at an angle of one-third.

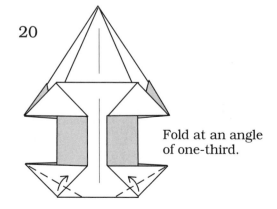

21

22

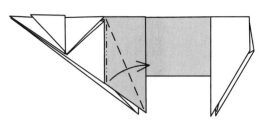

Crimp-fold.

23

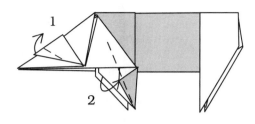

1. Outside-reverse-fold.
2. Tuck, repeat behind.

24

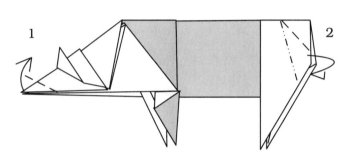

1. Outside-reverse-fold.
2. Crimp-fold.

25

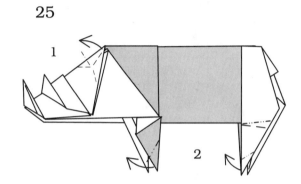

1. Rabbit-ear.
2. Reverse folds.
Repeat behind.

26

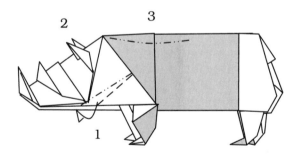

1. Shape the neck.
2. Open the ears.
3. Shape the back.
Repeat behind.

27

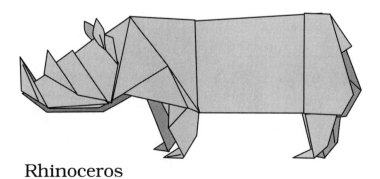

Rhinoceros

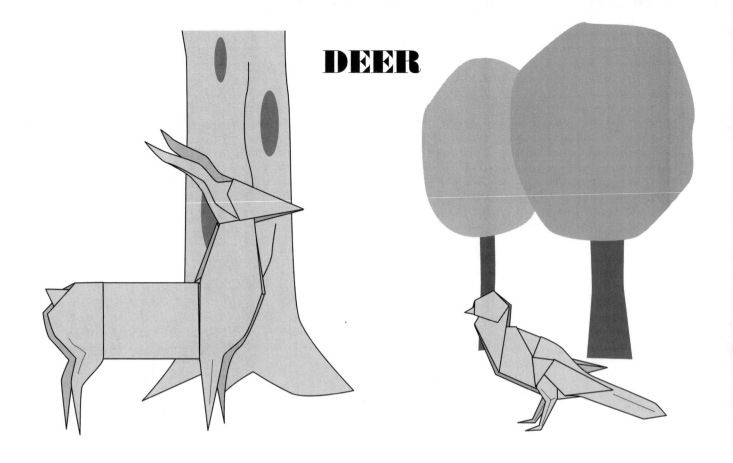

DEER

1

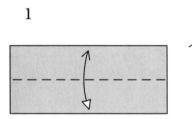

Fold and unfold.

2

3

Unfold.

4

5

6

7

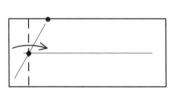

Unfold.

8

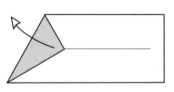

Squash-fold.

9

10

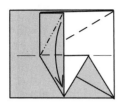

11

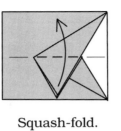

Squash-fold.

12

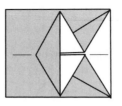

13

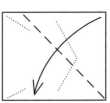

14

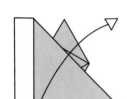

Unfold.

15

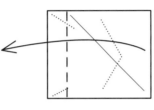

16

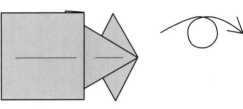

17

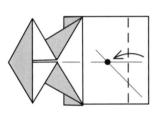

18

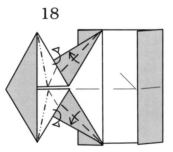

19

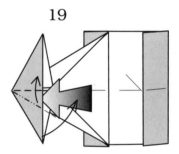

Squash-fold.

20

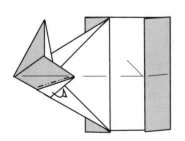

Squash-fold.

21

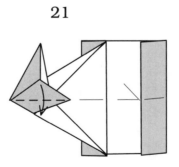

22

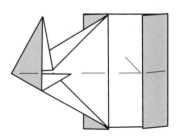

Repeat steps 19–21
on the top.

23

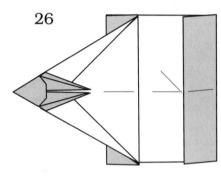

Petal-fold.

24

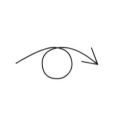

25

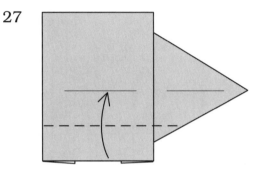

26

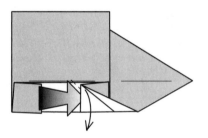

27

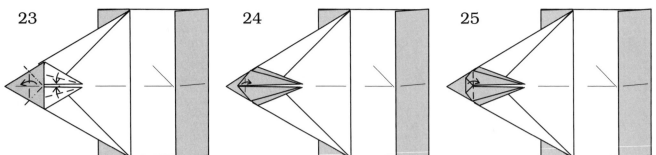

28

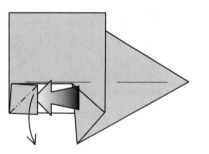

Squash-fold.

29

Squash-fold.

30

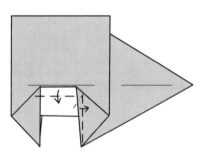

Squash-fold.

31

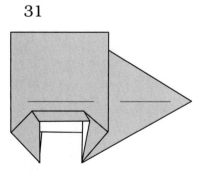

Repeat steps 27–30
on the top.

32

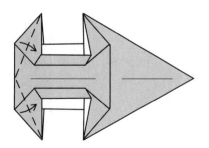

33

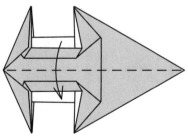

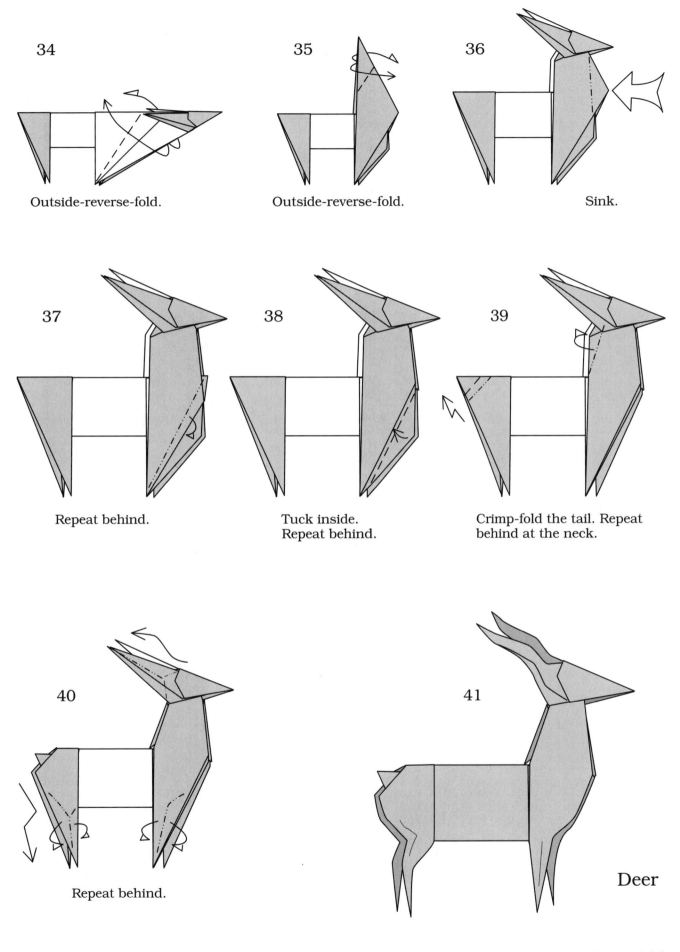

34

Outside-reverse-fold.

35

Outside-reverse-fold.

36

Sink.

37

Repeat behind.

38

Tuck inside.
Repeat behind.

39

Crimp-fold the tail. Repeat behind at the neck.

40

Repeat behind.

41

Deer

CAMEL

1

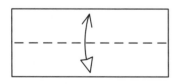

Fold and unfold.

2

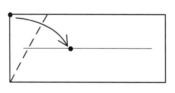

3

4

Unfold.

5

Unfold.

6

7

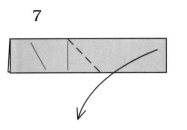

8

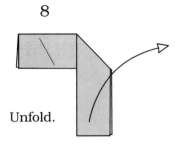

Unfold.

9

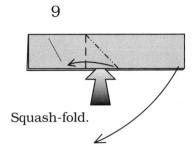

Squash-fold.

10

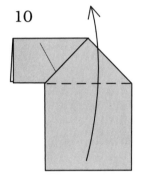

11

12

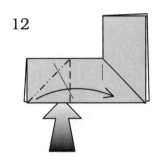

Squash-fold.

13

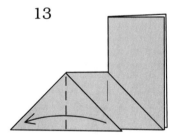

14

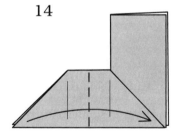

15

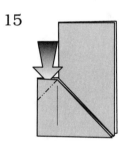

Reverse-fold.

16

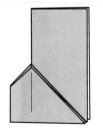

17

Squash-fold
behind.

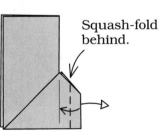

18

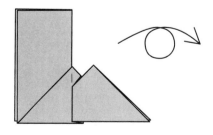

Camel 107

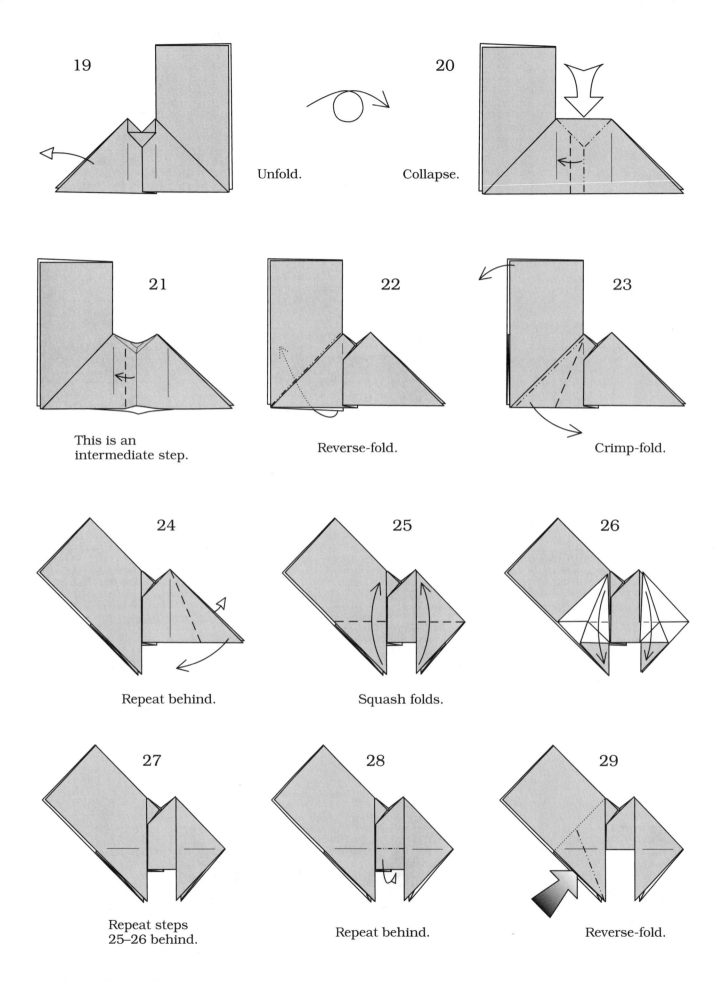

19

Unfold.

20

Collapse.

21

This is an
intermediate step.

22

Reverse-fold.

23

Crimp-fold.

24

Repeat behind.

25

Squash folds.

26

27

Repeat steps
25–26 behind.

28

Repeat behind.

29

Reverse-fold.

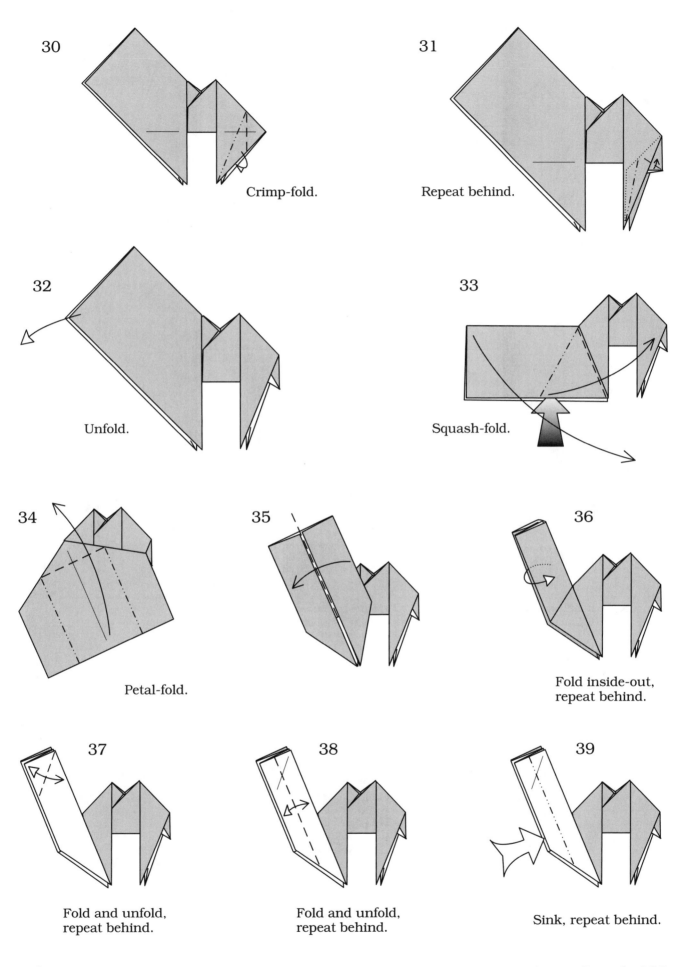

30

Crimp-fold.

31

Repeat behind.

32

Unfold.

33

Squash-fold.

34

Petal-fold.

35

36

Fold inside-out,
repeat behind.

37

Fold and unfold,
repeat behind.

38

Fold and unfold,
repeat behind.

39

Sink, repeat behind.

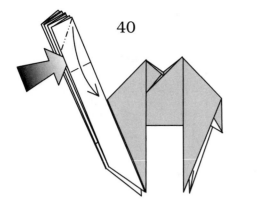

40

Stretch to fold the
ear. Repeat behind.

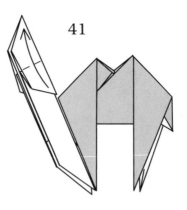

41

Repeat behind.

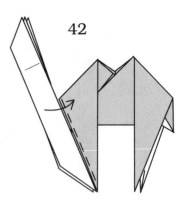

42

Repeat behind.

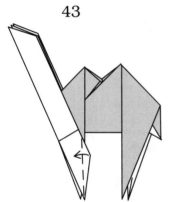

43

Repeat behind.

44

Outside-reverse-fold.

45

Unfold.

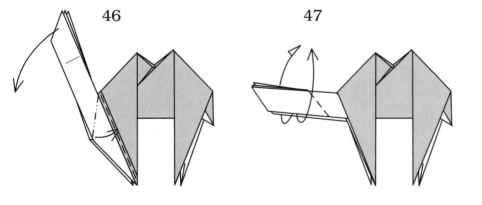

46

Tuck inside.

47

Outside-reverse-fold.

48

Outside-reverse-fold.

49

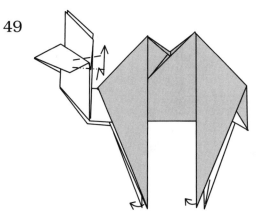

Simple mountain and valley
folds for the ears. Make the
hooves round. Repeat behind.

50

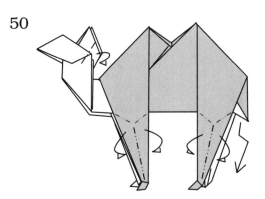

Repeat behind.

51

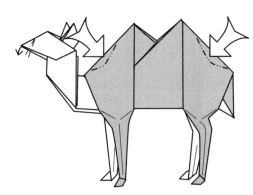

Make a tiny crimp
at the head.

52

Camel

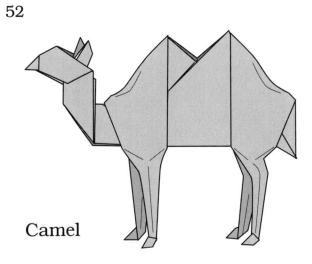

GIRAFFE

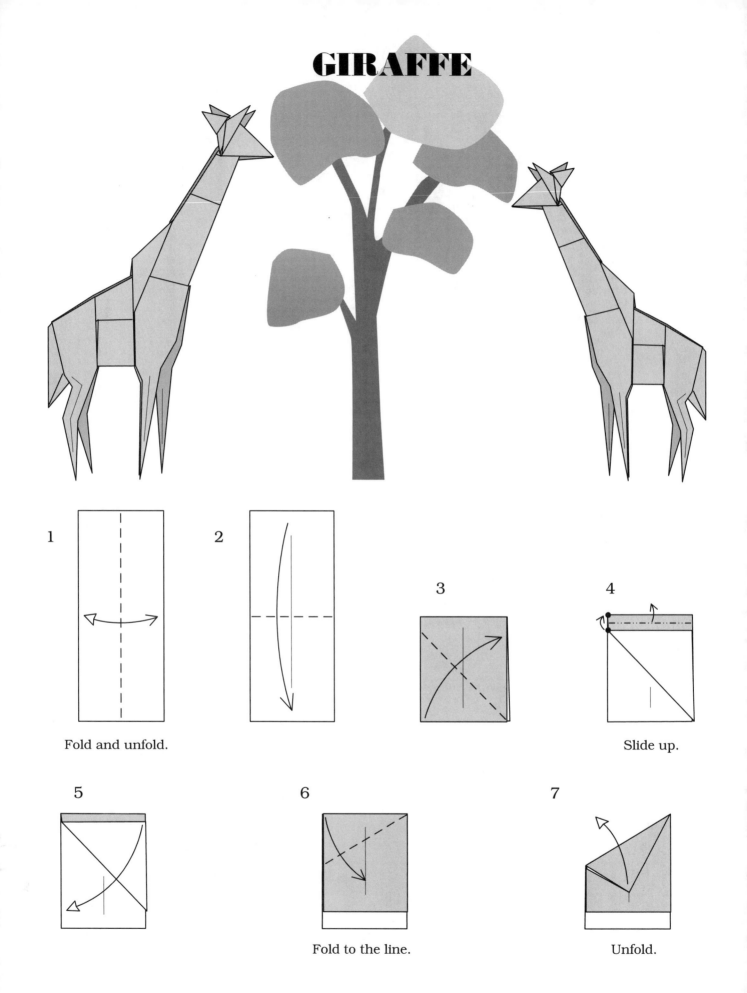

1 Fold and unfold.

2

3

4 Slide up.

5

6 Fold to the line.

7 Unfold.

8
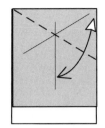

Fold and unfold.

9
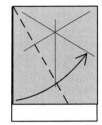

10
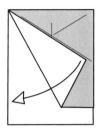

Unfold.

11
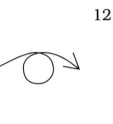

Fold and unfold.

12
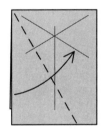

13
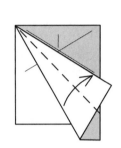

14
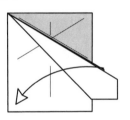

Unfold.

15

Repeat steps 12–14
on the right.

16
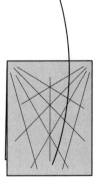

Unfold.

17
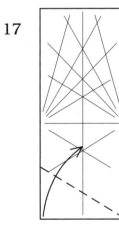

18
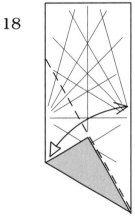

Fold and unfold.

19

Unfold.

20

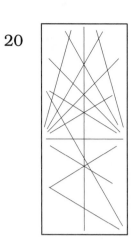

Repeat steps 17–19
on the right.

21

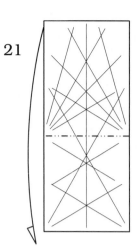

22

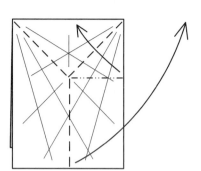

Rabbit-ear.

23

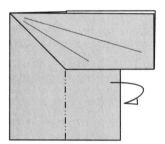

24

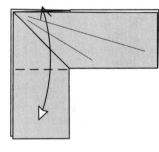

Fold and unfold,
then rotate.

25

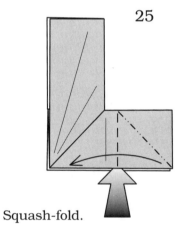

Squash-fold.

26

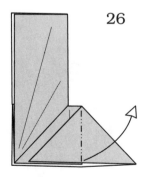

Unfold.

27

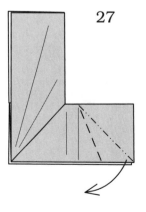

Crimp-fold.

28

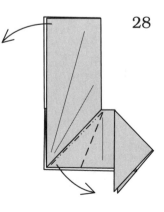

Crimp-fold.

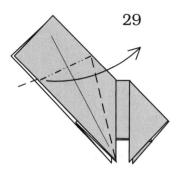

29

Squash-fold.

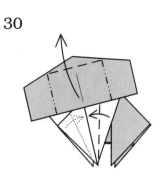

30

Petal-fold.

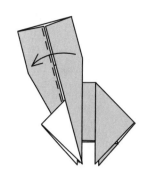

31

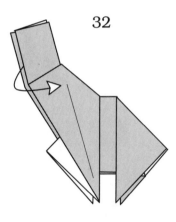

32

Fold inside-out,
repeat behind.

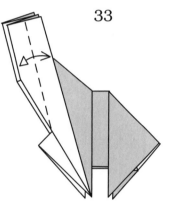

33

Fold and unfold,
repeat behind.

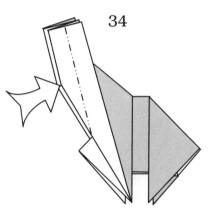

34

Sink, repeat
behind.

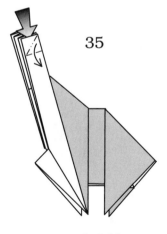

35

Squash-fold,
repeat behind.

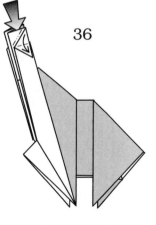

36

Squash-fold,
repeat behind.

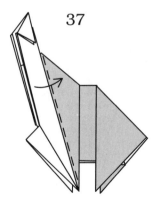

37

Repeat behind.

Giraffe 115

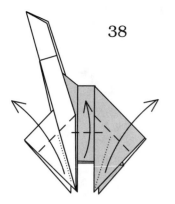

38

Open along
existing creases.

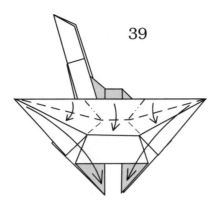

39

Close while
thinning the legs.

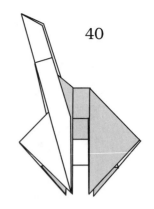

40

Repeat steps
38–39 behind.

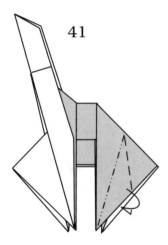

41

Crimp-fold.

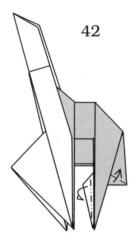

42

Squash-fold,
repeat behind.

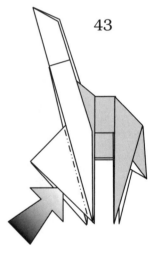

43

Reverse-fold.

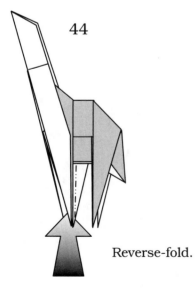

44

Reverse-fold.

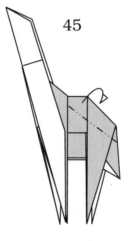

45

Fold behind.

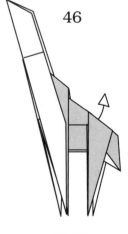

46

Unfold.

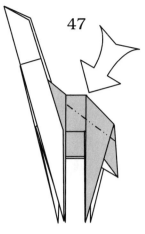

47

Sink.

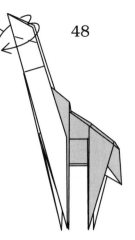

48

Outside-reverse-fold.

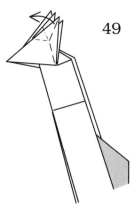

49

Rabbit-ear,
repeat behind.

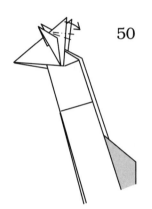

50

Repeat behind.

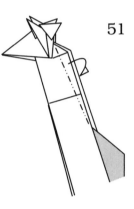

51

Repeat behind.

52

1. Crimp-fold.
2. Thin the legs.
3. Thin and bend the legs.
Repeat behind.

1

2

3

53

Giraffe

BASIC FOLDS

Rabbit Ear.

To fold a rabbit ear, one corner is folded in half and laid down to a side.

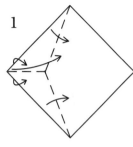
1

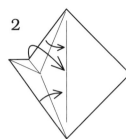
2

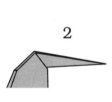
3

Fold a rabbit ear.

A three-dimensional intermediate step.

Double Rabbit Ear.

If you were to bend a straw you would be folding the double rabbit ear.

1
2

(Straw)

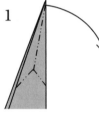
1

2

Make a double rabbit ear.

Squash Fold.

In a squash fold, some paper is opened and then made flat. The shaded arrow shows where to place your finger.

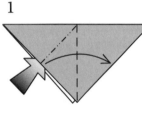
1

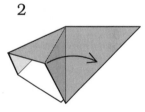
2

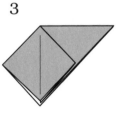
3

Squash-fold.

A three-dimensional intermediate step.

Petal Fold.

In a petal fold, one point is folded up while two opposite sides meet each other.

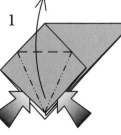
1

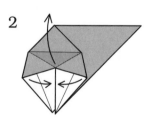
2

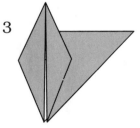
3

Petal-fold.

A three-dimensional intermediate step.

Inside Reverse Fold.

In an inside reverse fold, some paper is folded between layers. Here are two examples.

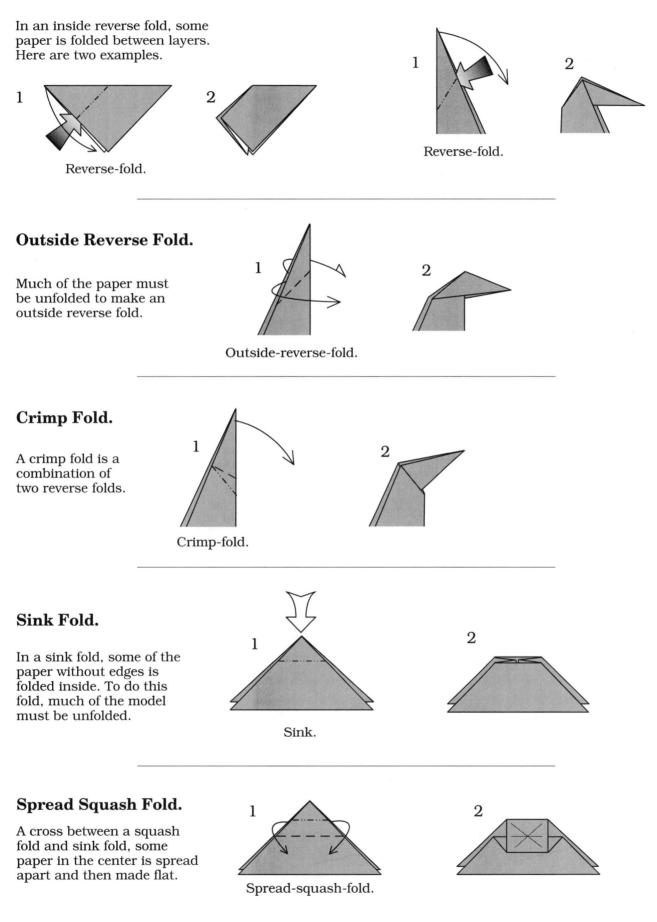

Reverse-fold.

Reverse-fold.

Outside Reverse Fold.

Much of the paper must be unfolded to make an outside reverse fold.

Outside-reverse-fold.

Crimp Fold.

A crimp fold is a combination of two reverse folds.

Crimp-fold.

Sink Fold.

In a sink fold, some of the paper without edges is folded inside. To do this fold, much of the model must be unfolded.

Sink.

Spread Squash Fold.

A cross between a squash fold and sink fold, some paper in the center is spread apart and then made flat.

Spread-squash-fold.